SPEAK AND READ
CHINESE

SPEAK AND READ CHINESE

Fun Mnemonic Devices for Remembering Chinese Words and Their Tones

Larry Herzberg

Stone Bridge Press • *Berkeley, California*

Published by
Stone Bridge Press
P. O. Box 8208, Berkeley, CA 94707
TEL 510-524-8732 • sbp@stonebridge.com • www.stonebridge.com

Printed in the United States of America.

p-ISBN 978-1-61172-031-0
e-ISBN 978-1-61172-921-4

CONTENTS

PREFACE

In studying eight foreign languages over many decades, I discovered that the best way for me to learn new vocabulary in those language was to think of mnemonic devices, i.e., memory hooks, for each word. I discovered that if I could relate the sound or meaning of a word I was trying to learn to a word in English, I stood a much better chance of cementing that word in my memory.

Using mnemonic devices to learn new vocabulary is not so crucial for an English speaker trying to learn a Romance language, given that 60% of words in French, Spanish, and Italian have English-language cognates. However, in a language as different from English as Chinese, it is most helpful to have clever ways at your disposal to jog your memory when trying to learn new vocabulary.

When I was first learning words like *piányi* (inexpensive), it helped to think about how clothing at J.C. Penney is inexpensive. It was also easy to remember the word *chē* (car), since the *ch* sounded like a car chugging along the highway. And the Chinese word *mǎi* (to buy) was much easier to recall if I thought about going into a store and thinking, "My, oh my, the high prices of things I want to buy!"

I don't have particularly catchy memory hooks for every single word in Chinese. And even if I did, I could never fit them all into this book. What I have done instead is to give mnemonic devices for approximately 300 commonly used Chinese words that all students learn in the first year or two of studying Chinese. I hope that these will encourage you to think of your own mnemonic devices for the words I do not include.

I have been teaching Chinese at the college level for thirty-seven years. When some years ago I anonymously surveyed nearly a hundred of my Chinese-language students as to how helpful they thought my mnemonic devices were, nearly 100% of them answered that they found them either very helpful or somewhat helpful. Only one student responded that he/she found them slightly annoying. I have, therefore, continued to use them in my teaching and hope to share them with a wider audience.

I do want to share a few words of caution about using mnemonics to remember vocabulary. First, these are just whimsical creations that have absolutely no etymological basis. Second, mnemonic devices, or "demonic devices" as some of my students have called them, cannot be relied upon for exact pronunciation. For that you have to try to mimic your Chinese teacher, your Chinese friends, and the native speakers in the listening exercises that you do for your class. My encouraging you to remember the word for Japan, Rìběn, by thinking of Japan as an "urban" country, might help you learn the word. But "urban" is hardly an exact guide to proper Chinese pronunciation.

I have yet to encounter another Chinese teacher who uses mnemonic devices to help students remember Chinese words. Most likely that is because most Chinese language teachers are native speakers of the language. They have been listening to and speaking in Chinese from the time they were infants and see no reason why anyone would need tricks to learn words that they acquired with their mother's milk. A non-native speaker like me who learned the Chinese language as an adult, however, understands well the difficulty of remembering words in a language that is so incredibly different from English.

Not only am I aware of no other teachers or textbooks that provide mnemonic devices for learning new vocabulary in Chinese, likewise I do not know of any resources that give clues as to how to remember the tones. In many Chinese-language classrooms students are simply expected to repeat words with the correct tones over and over until they have memorized them. This is, of course, important to do. The more you hear Chinese words spoken by native speakers with the correct tones, the easier it will be for you to remember them. Eventually, like native speakers of Chinese who do not have to think whether a word is first, second, third, or fourth tone, teachers hope you too will say words with correct tones as second nature.

For non-native speakers, however, learning the correct tone for every word is not an easy matter. I have, therefore, attempted to give helpful hints as to how you might remember the tones for the approximately 300 words included in this book. But remember, we can't consult early Chinese dynasties to discover why Chinese say each word with a particular intonation. These are just tricks to help you remember. For instance, the fact that the word for "high" or "tall," *gāo*, is said with a high, level tone (first tone) makes complete sense. Similarly, the fact that *diào*, "to drop," and *guà*, "to hang," are both said with the falling tone (fourth tone) is also very understandable. That words for things like "horse" (*mǎ*), and "chair" (*yǐ*) are said with the low rising tone (third tone) is logical, since a horse and a chair are things that you sit down on. It is also not surprising that almost all question words in Chinese, such as *shénme* (what?), *shéi* (who?), *zěnme* (how?), and *nǎr/nǎlǐ* (where?) are all said with a tone that rises, namely either the second or third tone, since this is the same questioning intonation we use in English.

The reasons why certain words in Chinese are spoken with certain tones have been lost in the fog of ancient history. The mnemonic devices I have provided in this book to help you remember tones may sometimes appear to be a real stretch. However, I trust that at least some of them might help you as you struggle to learn the tones of the various words. Please remember that the most important way to remember them is to listen to native speakers and to repeat what they say to yourself as many times as you can. Also remember that if you don't know the tone, you don't know the word! There is an important difference between the words *mǎi* (to buy) and *mài* (to sell). Similarly there is a huge difference between *wèn* (to ask), *wén* (to sniff), and *wěn* (to kiss)!

In addition to the mnemonic devices I have provided for spoken words and their tones, I have also provided mnemonics for characters. There are books that give the actual etymology of a great number of Chinese characters. There are other books that give tricks for remembering characters in creative ways that have nothing to do with their actual origin. In this book I have tried to provide both the correct etymology, should that be known, as well as my own fun and hopefully helpful tricks for remembering how to read and write various characters.

Traditional and simplified versions of the Chinese characters

There are currently two different versions of many of the Chinese characters. Chinese in Taiwan, Hong Kong, as well as those in the U.S. and Canada continue to use the "traditional" form of the characters as they have been written for the past several millennia. However, in the 1950s the Chinese in Mainland China began using "simplified" forms of many of the characters in order to promote literacy. Most students of the Chinese language in the U.S. and Canada only learn the simplified versions of the characters, since those characters are used by the 1.35 billion people living in Mainland China.

This book, however, includes both forms of the characters, when there are both traditional and simplified versions. There are two reasons for this. One reason is that we wish to honor those students whose parents are from either Taiwan or Hong Kong, and who elect to study only the traditional forms. The other reason is that the traditional forms of the characters in many cases reveal how the simplified forms were created, which is often as a skeletal outline of the original. More importantly the traditional forms show more clearly the etymology of the characters, which gives us insight into Chinese thought and culture, and, because of their greater detail, are in fact sometimes easier to remember. For that reason we have listed the traditional characters first.

If you're studying simplified characters, we suggest you still look at the traditional versions to help imprint in your memory the mnemonic devices we provide.

Radicals and phonetics

Every Chinese character contains at least one "radical," which is a simple picture that helps to show the general meaning of that character. For example, the "water" radical, written as 水, usually abbreviated and placed on the left side of a character, is found in all words that are either bodies of water (河 "river"; 湖 "lake"), or that have something to do with water, such as the character for "thirsty," written as 渴.

The "tree" radical is found in all characters that are either names of trees (松 "pine"; 李 "plum tree") or words for things made of wood (床 "bed"; 椅 "chair"). The "radical" is often found on the left side of a character but sometimes appears on the right side, the top, or the bottom of a character. There are 214 radicals in all, 100 of which account for nearly 99% of all characters.

Approximately 90% of Chinese characters currently in use also contain another type of pictograph that gives a hint as to the pronunciation of the character. These are called "phonetics." They are often characters by themselves, but are written as parts of more complex characters to help give the reader a clue to the pronunciation. For example, in the character for "ocean," written as 洋, the "water" radical is on the left side, signifying that the character has to do with water. The right side has the character for "sheep," written as 羊, as the phonetic, since the word for "sheep," *yáng*, is pronounced the same as the word for "ocean," *yáng*. This is an example of a perfect phonetic, which has the same pronunciation, including the same tone, as the entire character. Most likely all the phonetics were perfect when they were introduced into the language around 1,800 years ago, but over time the spoken language has continued to evolve, and many of the phonetics now only give us hints as to the pronunciation of the character as a whole.

Part of the brilliance of the Chinese written language is that phonetics often contribute to the meaning of a character, as well as give a clue as to pronunciation. For example, in the character 忘 wàng, "to forget," the "heart" radical 心 is on the bottom of the character, indicating that the character has to do with emotions or thought. The top part has the character for "death," 亡 wáng, as the phonetic. Beyond serving as a mere clue to pronunciation, this particular character was chosen as a phonetic because the intended metaphor is that to forget something is literally to have a thought die in the heart or mind.

*   *   *

I hope this slim volume will serve as a good supplement to whatever other resources you are using to learn Chinese. I also hope that you will continue to study a language so vital for Americans, Canadians, and other Westerners to learn. As China's importance in the world increases, its relationship with Western countries will only grow.

Larry Herzberg
Professor of Chinese
Calvin College
Grand Rapids, Michigan

COMMON CHINESE WORDS

ài   愛/爱   love

*Sometimes you **eye** somebody and fall in <u>love</u> with them and then **ay, yay, yay** the consequences!*

ài is fourth tone/falling tone, since you ***fall*** in love with someone.

愛   The traditional character shows a hand on top reaching in for someone's heart, the character 心, through a roof. This roof is the metaphoric barrier we all keep around our hearts for fear of getting hurt. The person whose love is being sought reciprocates by offering up their heart with both hands to the hand reaching in for love.

爱   In the simplified character, the heart and two hands under the roof are replaced by two hands locked in friendship.

ānpái   安排   to arrange

*When you bake a pie and invite over guests, you have to <u>arrange</u> what you're going to put **on** the **pie**. Ice cream or whipped cream?*

ān is first tone/high level tone, since you arrange things by putting them ***flat*** on the table. *pái* is second tone/rising tone, since you ask your guests, with questioning intonation, would you like some ***pie***?

安   This character shows a woman under the roof arranging things for the party.

排   This character consists of a hand on the left lining the guests up at either side of the table.

bái 白 white

*When an army runs up the <u>white</u> flag, they're saying **bye, bye** to any hope of victory.*

bái is second tone/rising tone, since when asking about ethnicity, a pollster, and certainly a racist, might ask with a questioning intonation "white?"

白 The character shows the sun coming up at the break of day. The top stroke shows the rising of the sun at dawn. The original idea was the "whiteness" of the sun, and has come to mean "white" as well as "fair-skinned."

bǎi 百 (a) hundred

*That's a great **buy** for a <u>hundred</u> dollars!*

bǎi is third tone/low rising tone, since a hundred ounces of gold in your pocket would certainly sink deep down into it!

百 This character has the character for "one," 一 as the radical on top, indicating units of ones, tens, hundreds, etc.

bān 搬 to move (place of residence or furniture)

*When you <u>move</u>, it's helpful to have a moving **ban** (van)!*

bān is first tone/high level tone, since when you move things, you try to keep them level and not let them tip over.

搬 The character has the "hand" radical on the left, since we use our hands to move things. The phonetic on the right shows a boat on the left being moved or "poled" by two hands on the right, which was the traditional way of navigating a boat down a river or lake.

bàn 辦/办 to handle/manage (something)

One way to <u>handle</u> *a matter, if you're in a position of authority, is to* **<u>ban</u>** *(prohibit) it.*

bàn is fourth tone/falling tone, since you need to handle matters decisively and speak with decisive intonation.

辦/办 The traditional character actually shows two criminals with hands and feet in manacles on either side, being handled with force, which in Chinese is the character 力. The simplified character shows handling matters with energy or force, with what appears to be a drop of sweat on either side.

bànfǎ 辦法/办法 method; way (to do something)

One <u>way</u> *to keep warm is to make a* **<u>bonfire</u>** *(bànfǎ).*

bàn is said with the fourth tone/falling tone and means "to handle/manage." When you are managing things, you have to do so confidently, and so the authoritative fourth tone seems appropriate. **fǎ** is said with the third tone/low rising tone and means "way; method." When you manage things, you must do so thoroughly, from top to bottom. Hence *bànfǎ* is said with a falling tone followed by a low tone.

辦/办 The traditional character actually shows two criminals with hands and feet in manacles on either side, being handled with force, which in Chinese is the character 力. The simplified character shows handling matters with energy or force, with what appears to be a drop of sweat on either side.

法 By itself this character means "law" or "way." The character shows water on the left and the character 去, meaning "to go," on the right. The true etymology of this word comes from the Chinese belief that just as water runs in certain channels, human behavior should be guided in certain channels by the rule of law.

bāngmáng 帮忙/幫忙 to help/assist

*I get a **bang** out of <u>helping</u> my fellow **man** (and fellow woman).*

bāng is first tone/high level tone, since you hope the person who helps you will be on the level. **_máng_** is second tone/rising tone, since when asking for help, it's with a rising or questioning intonation: "help?"

幫 The traditional version of this character seems to show earth or dirt piled up in a trench on the top left, with a hand bleeding on the top right; as the guns go off, "bang, bang," you raise the white flag, the "cloth" radical on the bottom, 巾, shouting "help, help!"

帮 Think of this simplified form as a big guy on the top right holding a weapon or tool on the top left, coming to help when he sees a flag being waved. The top part of the simplified character is actually a phonetic, meaning "confederation."

忙 This character means "a favor" or "busy." It shows the "heart" radical on the left is occupied, with the character for "coffin" on the right as a phonetic, warning about the danger of getting too busy!

bāngzhù 帮助/幫助 to help/assist

*I get a **bang** out of <u>helping</u> **you**!*

bāng is first tone/high level tone, since you hope the person who helps you will be on the level. **_zhù_** is fourth tone/falling tone, giving the end of the compound word for "help" an affirming, decisive sound, indicating a strong desire to be of assistance.

助 The character means "to aid or assist." It shows the "energy"/"strength" radical on the right, since you need to use energy or strength to assist others. The phonetic on the right can be seen in the Chinese word 姐姐, meaning "older sister."

bāo 包 to wrap up

*The clerks in the store might **bow** to you before they <u>wrap up</u> your purchase and put a red bow on it.*

bāo is first tone/high level tone, since you need to put a package on a level surface before wrapping it.

包 The character seems to show an embryo wrapped in the womb, but most likely shows a person with their arms wrapped around some object.

bǎo 飽/饱 full (from eating)

<u>**bǎo**</u> *resembles the sound of a burp when a person is <u>full</u>.*

bǎo is third tone/low rising tone, since you feel full because food has settled down into your stomach.

飽 The character has the "food" radical on the left, showing a hand on top feeding from a rice bowl in the middle and using a spoon or ladle on the bottom to eat with. The character 包 is the phonetic on the right, seeming to add to the meaning by appearing to show the head and bent leg of a person sitting and feeling full after eating. The top strokes emphasize fullness by enclosing the person.

bào (bàozhǐ) 報/报 newspaper, report

<u>**bào**</u> *sounds like the barking of a dog (bow wow) when the <u>newspaper</u> boy tries to deliver the newspaper.*

bào is fourth tone/falling tone since the word is also the verb "to report," something that must be done with a decisive tone to the voice.

報 The character actually shows a criminal on the left, with a head on top and hands and legs in chains, being reported on in court by an official holding a staff (top right) in the hand (bottom right). It originally meant to report on someone. The simplified character substitutes a hand on the left.

bǎobǎo 寶寶/宝宝 baby; little treasure

*"When the **bough** breaks, the **baby** will fall," and down will come **baobao**, cradle and all.*

bǎobǎo is third tone/low rising tone, as the baby settles down into the cradle to sleep.

寶/宝 Since this character written once means "treasure," the traditional version of the character actually shows three things of value in ancient China, namely jade, pottery, and cowry shells, all kept secure under a roof. The simplified version only has the "jade" radical under the roof. The compound for baby literally means "treasure-treasure."

běi 北 north

*Hudson **Bay** is way up **north** in Canada.*

běi is third tone/low rising tone, since the water in a **bay** goes down quite deep.

北 Since Chinese homes are ideally built with southern exposure for maximum sunlight, the master of the house would sit with his back to the north whenever he invited guests to his home. That way he would see when they arrived and could get up to greet them.

bēizi 杯子 cup; glass

*Whether you fill your glass with **bay** rum or put **bay** leaves in your tea, **bēizi** is a **glass** or **cup**.*

bēizi is first tone/high level tone, since you need to keep your glass high and level to keep whatever is inside from spilling.

杯 The "tree" radical is on the left, since cups were originally made out of wood. The phonetic on the right is 不.

子 This character is a suffix that was added in the modern language and is a common ending on nouns.

běn 本 root; origin; measure word for books

Just as a **bun** *is the root or base of a hamburger, so is a book the* <u>root</u> *or* <u>origin</u> *of learning.*

běn is third tone/low rising tone since the root of the tree is down low, at the bottom of the tree.

> 本 The small horizontal line at the bottom of the "tree" radical emphasizes the root of the tree. The actual etymology is that books are the root or origin of learning.

bèn 笨 stupid; dumb; clumsy

<u>*"Buns"*</u> *are another slang work for "ass," and you have to admit that some people are really just* <u>dumb</u> *asses!*

bèn is fourth tone/falling tone, since clumsy people often fall down. And when you accuse a person of being stupid, you're going to say it with a decisive intonation, i.e., a falling tone.

> 笨 The character has the "bamboo" radical on the top, with the character 本 on the bottom as the phonetic. The swaying from side to side of bamboo in a strong wind seemed an apt metaphor for clumsiness and, by extension, stupidity.

bǐ 比 to compare; compared with …

<u>*"B"*</u> *students inevitably* <u>compare</u> *themselves to "A" students.*

bǐ is third tone/low rising tone because when comparing yourself to others you should always lower your voice out of humility.

> 比 The character shows two people sitting side by side, comparing their respective heights.

bǐ 筆/笔   writing instrument (brush, pen, pencil, etc.)

---

*A **Bic** pen is a <u>writing instrument</u> with which to write your ABCs.*

bǐ is third tone/low rising, since you must lower the pen or pencil down to the surface of the paper on which you are writing.

筆/笔   The original meaning of this character was "brush," so both the traditional and simplified versions show the radical for "bamboo" on top, from which the handle of the brush is made. The traditional character shows the hand holding a writing brush. The simplified version simply shows the character 毛 , meaning "hair" and representing the goat's hair or camel's hair that make up the bristles of the brush.

bié 别   don't; other/another

<u>Don't</u> **be** a "**B**" student! **Be** an "A" student!
<u>Other</u> students may get a "**B**," but you strive to get an "A"!

bié is a second tone/rising tone. While it seems like **bié** should be fourth tone/falling tone when commanding someone to not do something, it is instead second tone/rising tone. However, we question being told to not do something by asking "Don't?!" with questioning, rising intonation.

别   The "knife" radical is on the right, as if to say "Cut it out! Don't do that!" The left side has the "mouth" radical on top of the "energy" radical, as if adding force to one's words when saying, "Don't!"

The actual etymology has much more to do with the original meaning of this character, which meant other or another. The knife shows that something is being cut away or being "othered," while the "energy" radical under the "mouth" radical on the left shows that in addition to verbal persuasion, force is also being applied.

bǐjìběn 筆記本/笔记本 notebook

*Big fans of the **Bee Gees** kept <u>notebooks</u> of pictures and other mementos of Bee Gees concerts.*

bǐjìběn is said with third/low rising tone, followed by a fourth/falling tone, ending with another third/low rising tone. The effect is much like the motion of a pen moving downward, then upward, then downward again as it takes notes.

記/记 For the traditional character the "speech" radical on the left reflects the writing down or recording of what was said. The phonetic on the right is 己, meaning "self," and shows a silkworm curled up on itself. The simplified character is the same, except the "speech" radical has been simplified.

bìng 病 illness; disease; sick (both a noun and adjective)

<u>Bing</u> *Crosby, the famous crooner, was <u>sick</u> ... very <u>sick</u> ... and then he died!*

bìng is said with the fourth tone/falling tone, since sickness falls upon us unawares. The power of illness to affect us also makes it logical that the word is said with the decisive fourth tone.

病 The character on the right side looks like a person enclosed in a room wearing a nightcap. The left and top parts of the character show the body as a temple, with a roof and sidewall. The two little skewed lines on the far left show germs assailing the body.

In reality, the character has the "sickness" radical on the left, which some of my students describe as a bed, with the two feet of the patient sticking out on the far left and a hot water bottle on the very top. 丙, which is the third of the ten Heavenly Stems, is the phonetic on the right, which is actually an axe-head turned upside down.

bìxū   必須/必须   must; need to

We Americans are quite a litigious people, who seem to feel the <u>*need to*</u> ***be su****ing people all the time!*

bì is said with the fourth tone/falling tone, since when you're told you must do something, it's always said with a decisive falling tone.

xū is said with the first tone/high level tone, as the person insisting you do something levels off her or his voice.

必   This character seems to show the radical for "heart" being split in two by the long, fairly vertical line that goes from top right to bottom left. To truly know what love is, you <u>**must**</u> have had your heart broken at least once.

須/须   On the right is a character that looks like a head, with the lines on the left looking like the worries that <u>**must**</u> plague us, it seems, as part of the human condition.

bù   不   no; not; don't

It's <u>*not*</u> *nice to say "*<u>**boo**</u>*" when it's* <u>*not*</u> *Halloween! So* <u>*don't*</u> *say "*<u>**boo.**</u>*"*

bù is fourth tone/falling tone. It makes sense that a decisive word like "no" or "not" would be said with a decisive, falling intonation.

不   The true etymology is said to be a bird trying to fly up to the sky but being blocked by some obstacle, such as the overhang of a roof. The vertical line is the body of the bird, with the wings on either side. The horizontal line shows the obstacle blocking the bird from flying upward.

búbì 不必 no need to; don't have to

---

*You don't have to hire someone who's a **booby**!*

bù and **bì** are fourth tone/falling tone, as you'd expect from words with decisive meanings. However, whenever there are two characters in a compound that are both falling tones, the first character is said with rising intonation. It's what automatically happens to your voice when quickly saying two falling tones in a row.

不 The true etymology is said to be a bird trying to fly up to the sky but being blocked by some obstacle, such as the overhang of a roof. The vertical line is the body of the bird, with the wings on either side. The horizontal line shows the obstacle blocking the bird from flying upward.

必 This character seems to show the radical for "heart" being split in two by the long, fairly vertical line that goes from top right to bottom left. To truly know what love is, you **must** have had your heart broken at least once. What the character really shows is an arrow striking a target right in the center, which was necessary to win an archery contest.

cài 菜 vegetables; food/cuisine; dishes (entrees)

The Chinese eat more vegetables as a percentage of their diet than the people of almost any other culture. They enjoy eating vegetables because they know how to make them tasty, by cooking them in the wok in a little bit of oil and adding various delicious sauces. They also don't overcook vegetables so that they "lack soul." Americans, on the other hand, tend to not like vegetables and as many as a third of Americans go an entire day without eating a single vegetable, in large part because we don't know how to cook them properly. All this is by way of saying that when

Americans are served vegetables instead of meat or French fries,
*they may be heard to say: "It's, **sigh,** only vegetables!"*

cài is said with the fourth tone/falling tone. When you sigh, the
motion of your body is in a downward direction. It therefore
makes sense that this word would be pronounced with the falling
tone, at least in the world of mnemonic devices.

菜　On top is, of course, the "grass" radical, which is the radical on top of a great many characters for various vegetables,
as well as for flowers and herbs. Beneath it is the phonetic
that seems to show a hand pulling out a plant, in this case the
"tree" radical, from the ground, like a carrot or turnip.

cānguǎn　餐館/餐馆　restaurant

When you go to a restaurant you ask "What's on the menu and
*what are we **guanna** (**gonna**) order?"*

cān is first tone/high level tone. The food in a restaurant is
always placed on a high, level table, after all. **guǎn** is third tone/
low rising tone. It's the suffix for a number of different buildings,
including library (图书馆), gym (体育馆), and museum (博物馆).
All of these are large buildings that need their foundations dug
deep, and so it perhaps makes sense that *guǎn* would be said with
the low rising tone.

餐　The top right part of the first character shows a hand
holding on the left a type of spoon. The "food" radical on the
bottom part of the character shows a hand on top scooping up
rice from a bowl beneath it, using another type of spoon on
the very bottom.

館/馆　The second character has the "food" radical on the
left side, with the phonetic 官, meaning "official," on the
right. The phonetic looks like a fat official, with a head and
large belly, dining under the roof of a restaurant. The true
etymology of the official phonetic is a depiction of the official
who guards the fortifications of a city, with the "roof" radical

on top and the strokes below it showing the building blocks of the city walls.

cānjiā 参加/參加 take part in; participate; join

Sanjay Gupta is a physician who often *takes part in* TV news shows.

Both characters in the compound *cānjiā* are first tone/high level tone, perhaps because when you join a group, everyone is ideally on the same level.

参/參 The traditional character shows three noses at the bottom consisting of three slanted lines, both of which indicate a joining together of many equal elements. The simplified version reduces the three noses on top to just one.

加 This character means "to add." It shows adding force, with the "energy" or "force" radical on the left, to one's words or verbal arguments, represented by the "mouth" radical on the right.

cāochǎng 操場/操场 athletic field

When you exercise or do sports, *it's how* you do it that matters. Do it wrong and the resul*t's "ow!"*
Play well on the *athletic field*, and you could end up a **chang**pion (champion)!

cāo is first tone/high level tone. Whether playing soccer, baseball, or running on a track on the athletic field, you're running on a level surface, so first tone makes some sense.

chǎng is third tone/low rising tone. When you're emphasizing the field itself, which is below your feet, perhaps the third tone is logical.

操/操 This character means "exercise" and has the "hand" radical on the left, since so many different sports involve using the hands. The phonetic on the right, with the three mouths on top and the "wood" radical on the bottom, can be seen as a crowd of cheering spectators sitting on bleachers made of wood.

場/场 This character means "field" and appropriately enough has the "earth" radical on the left. The phonetic on the right is found in many characters ending with the -ang sound. It shows the sun shooting down its rays on the ground, as it does on nice days on the athletic field.

chá 茶 tea

The caffeine in <u>tea</u> makes you want to "__cha-cha__"!

chá is said with the second tone/rising tone. When you serve tea, you offer it to your guest by asking, "Tea?" with a questioning or rising intonation.

茶 The character has the "grass" radical on top, which is the radical not only for flowers and vegetables, but also for many herbs. Below that is a sort of roof or protective shelter, under which the plucked leaves of the tea plant are being dried.

cháng 長/长 long

Think a <u>long</u> __chain__!

cháng is said with the second tone/rising tone. When the word is said slowly, in a drawn-out way and with the rising tone, it sounds like you are stretching out a piece of taffy. Try it!

長/长 The traditional character actually shows long flowing hair on the top, tied on the bottom with some sort of elaborate hairpin. The simplified character looks like a hair scrunchie turned sideways.

chángcháng 常常 often

*Very <u>often</u> words in Chinese are pronounced "qing," "<u>**chang**</u>," or "chung"!*

chángcháng is said with the second tone/rising tone, as if asking "Often? Not just sometimes?"

常 The character has 尚 on the top, a common phonetic. This phonetic depicts the slanted roof tiles and roof of a Chinese home over a window and is often seen in characters that end with the *-ang* sound.

The radical on the bottom is the "cloth" radical. The actual etymology is that a flag, made out of cloth, was always held up at the head of a marching army. This character originally meant "always," but has come to mean "often."

chángchang 嘗嘗/尝尝 to taste; to sample (food)

A homonym with the Chinese word for "often," this word sounds very much like someone chewing on something.

chángchang is said with the second tone/rising tone, as if you're moving your jaw upward in a chewing motion.

嘗 The traditional character has the same phonetic on top as 常常. The bottom part actually shows a finger being inserted into the mouth, looking very much like the "sun" radical, tasting something.

尝 The simplified character looks like a napkin on the top that's folded in the way some fancy restaurants will do, on top of the radical for "roof," which here might be thought to be the top of a table on which the napkin rests. Underneath the napkin on the table are two noses, which could be thought of as two diners sampling the food.

chànggē(r)　唱歌　to sing (literally: to sing songs)

---

*Some singers such as Gregorian monks **chant** their songs. And **Ger**bers baby food is so delicious, that babies <u>sing</u> out for it.*

chàng , the verb, is said with the fourth tone/falling tone, since when you begin to sing, you must do so with confidence, and the falling tone is the most decisive-sounding tone in Chinese.

gēr, the noun, is said with the first tone/high level tone. When you sing, you hold or elongate different notes. The first tone in Chinese is the longest, most drawn-out tone.

　唱歌　is actually a verb-object compound, which literally means "sing songs." The character 唱 shows a mouth on the left as the radical, since you open your mouth when you sing. The phonetic on the right seems to show two "suns," one on top of the other, but actually portrays two mouths filled with sound.

　歌　This character, meaning "song, " shows two mouths with breath rising up (欠) from each. The two mouths also serve as a phonetic, since they are a doubling of the character 可 (*kě*).

chǎo　炒　to stir-fry

---

*<u>chǎo</u>, <u>stir-fry</u>, is what Chinese do to their food before they **chow** down! When you say it, it also sounds like hot oil bubbling in the wok.*

chǎo is third tone/low rising tone, which makes sense since you drop the food down into the bottom of the wok to cook it.

　炒　The character has the "fire" radical on the left. Almost every character that has to do with cooking uses this radical, since we always heat food when cooking it.

chǎo 吵 noisy; loud

*Little **chow** dogs often are very yappy, <u>noisy</u> dogs. And people with poor table manners can be heard to **chow** down very <u>noisily</u>! Notice that the sound "ow!" is included in the word noisy. Loud sounds are "ow" or "ouch" to our ears.*

chǎo is a homonym with the word "to stir-fry" and also shares the third tone/low rising tone. When you drop oil down into the wok and heat it up, it makes a rather loud frying and popping sound. Perhaps that's why this *chǎo* is also said with the third tone.

吵 This character is written with the "mouth" radical on the left, indicating that this character has something to do with speech or noise. Like the character 炒, it also has 少 as the phonetic on the right, which means less. When people speak loudly, we do wish they would make less noise!

chāzi 叉子 fork

<u>Chā</u> is the sound of stabbing something with a <u>fork</u>.

chā is first tone, as is the word for "knife," dāozi. Perhaps this is because eating utensils like a knife and fork are placed flat on the table for diners to use.

叉 This character shows a large forked weapon, with the sharp points at the top of the character.

子 This character is a suffix that was added in the modern language and is a common ending on nouns.

chē (chē) 車/车 car

*Old <u>cars</u> will just **chug** down the highway.*

chē is first tone/high level tone, as befits a vehicle that moves horizontally.

車/车 The traditional character actually shows a cart, with the top and bottom horizontal strokes representing the wheels, the long vertical stroke showing the axle, and the middle section portraying the body of the cart, all from a bird's-eye view. The simplified character shows a bare-bones skeletal outline of the traditional character, which is how so many of the simplified characters were formed.

chéng 城 city

*A <u>city</u> is a big, **chunky** construct.*

chéng is said with the second tone/rising tone. Cities in the past were often built on a hill, for defensive purposes, so you would have to walk or ride up into the city. Hence the second tone seems appropriate.

城 The character has the "earth" radical on the left, indicating the clay or mud brick from which the walls of ancient halls were constructed. The character on the right is the phonetic character and includes a knife on the left, 刀, and a halberd on the right, 戈, indicating the weapons used to defend the city walls.

chī 吃 to eat

*Chocolaty, chewy, **chi**. Or think about <u>eating</u> **chur**ros!*

chī is first tone/high level tone, appropriate perhaps because you shovel food directly into your mouth, hopefully in a high, straight line.

吃 The character contains the "mouth" radical on the left, since we feed ourselves via the mouth. The phonetic on the right looks like a dribble running down a baby's chin as it eats. In fact it is the character 乞, which means "to beg," and shows someone kneeling, which they might do when asking for food on a cold day.

chòu 臭 to stink; stinky; smelly

*Ou**ch**, **oh**, so stinky it almost makes you **cho**-ke!*

chòu is said with the fourth tone/falling tone. When we call something "stinky" or "smelly," we generally say it with a decisive falling intonation.

臭 The character is written with the "nose" radical on top and a "dog" radical on the bottom. Dogs have a far greater sense of smell than humans, and are often attracted by things with a strong smell that people find repellent but that dogs find irresistible.

chuān 穿 to put on (clothing); to wear

*Ch**oose** whatever you **want** to **wear** and put it **on**!*

chuān is first tone/high level tone. We lay our clothes flat on a high surface to iron them before we put them on.

穿 The original meaning of this character is "to pierce." It shows the "cave" radical on top, 穴, symbolizing a hole made in cloth or some other surface. The radical on the bottom is for "canine tooth," 牙, which represents a sharp object piercing something to make a hole.

Since when you make a garment, you first have to pierce a piece of cloth with a needle, this character by extension went from meaning "to pierce" to meaning "to put on" or "to wear" the garment.

chúfáng 廚房/厨房 kitchen

*The <u>kitchen</u> is the room in the house where we do our **chew**ing, putting our **fangs** into the food to **chew** it.*

chú and *fáng* are said with the second tone/rising tone. After all, we do raise up the food from the stove and put it on our plates, so perhaps the rising tone is appropriate.

廚/厨 The traditional character version seems to show, under the roof, a hand on the right cooking with a pot on the stove. The opening of the pot is shown by 口, the "mouth" radical, with 土, the "earth" radical, seeming to represent the lid on the pot. Everything under the "roof" radical with the "side wall" radical 广 is actually a phonetic, with the "earth" radical removed in the simplified version.

房 This character is a suffix for many rooms in the house and is an abbreviation of the Chinese word for room, 房间. It shows the "door" radical 户, a radical formed by distorting the left side of the traditional character for door, namely 門.

chūntiān 春天 spring (the season)

*<u>Spring</u> is the **won**derful season when life springs up anew.*

The Chinese words for three of the four seasons of the year are said with the first tone/high level tone, including *chūn*. Perhaps that is because each season lasts three months and so deserves to be said with a long, drawn-out tone, i.e., the first tone.

春 This character actually shows plants at the top that appear to be coming out in spring under the influence of the sun, shown at the bottom.

天 In modern Chinese, the word for "day" is added to each of the names for the four seasons to avoid confusion with other homophonic characters. It's as if in English we didn't just say "spring or summer," but rather "spring days" or "summer days."

chūqù 出去 to go out

The Chattanooga **Choo-Choo** *goes out from the station.*

chū is first tone/high level tone and means "out." The feeling is that of coming straight out with what you want to say.

出去 Whereas in English we say "go out," the Chinese literally say "out go." The character 出 shows a plant coming out of the ground. The character 去, meaning "to go," appears to show the nose of a dog on the bottom going along the ground (top part) and sniffing something. The true etymology of the character, in its ancient form, actually shows the lid of a pot being removed, hence the idea of "taking away" and, by extension, "going."

chúshī 廚師/厨师 cook; chef

The food made by the *chef* **sure** *is the food you'd prefer to* **chew**!

chúshī is said with the first tone/high level tone because a teacher or "master" of something definitely possesses a high level of learning and ability.

廚/厨 The traditional character version seems to show, under the roof, a hand on the right cooking with a pot on the stove. The opening of the pot is shown by 口, the "mouth" radical, with 土, the "earth" radical, seeming to represent the lid on the pot. Everything under the "roof" radical with the "side wall" radical 广 is actually a phonetic, with the "earth" radical removed in the simplified version.

師/师 This character originally referred to the general who was in charge of guarding the walls of the city. Only later did it come to mean "master" or "teacher." The left side of the character shows the building blocks of a city wall. The right side is the character 市, meaning "city," and serves as a phonetic that contributes to the meaning. The character 市 includes the "cloth" radical on the bottom (巾), representing the cloth flags that marked the entry into the ancient cities of China. The simplified form on the left seems to show a very slender teacher in profile, while the right side has the teacher facing the class with arms held down at her/his side.

cì   次   time(s); occurrence(s)

It's how many times you practice something that determines how good you get.

cì is said with the fourth tone/falling tone. When you state how many times you've done something, it's usually said with a decisive falling tone to your voice.

次   The character appears to have the "ice" radical on the left, but in the ancient form was written as two skewed lines, representing doing something more than once. The right side shows a person on the bottom taking one breath after another, represented by the two lines on the top right showing the oscillation of the breath.

dà   大   big; large

*The **D.A.** is a big person in our legal system. And, for the Irish, "**Da**" is an informal, affectionate term for "Dad" or "father," a man big in the eyes of his children.*

dà is said with the fourth tone/falling tone. You would expect that a word meaning "big" would be said with a decisive falling intonation.

大   The character shows a person with their arms outstretched, as if bragging that the fish that got away was *that* big!

dàgài 大概 probably; approximately

*That **guy** was <u>probably</u> someone's "**Da**"!*

dàgài is said with fourth tones/falling tones.

You would expect a word that basically means "almost definite" to be said with assertive falling intonation.

大 The character shows a person with their arms outstretched, as if bragging that the fish that got away was <u>that</u> big!

概 This character has the "wood" radical on the left, since the original idea was measuring the approximate length of the wooden beams of a house. The phonetic on the right side seems to show a <u>guy</u> on the right, with his two legs on the bottom, holding something in his hand. The left side seems to show another <u>guy</u> looking at him, with his head turned in the other guy's direction and with his legs curled up in a sitting position.

dàifu 大夫 doctor

*A confident <u>doctor</u> whose patient is afraid he's terminally ill might say "<u>**Die**</u>? **Phoo**! You're not going to die! I'll cure you."*

dàifu is said with the fourth tone/falling tone. Doctors tend to be people with a high degree of confidence, so you might expect that the word for them would be said with a confident, assertive falling intonation.

大 Usually pronounced as *dà*, as in the word for "big," you can remember this character by recalling that doctors are a big help in the fight against disease.

夫 This character shows a powerful person with what appear to be two sets of arms, the better to help you.

dàizi 袋子 bag

A *bag* is what you should put used *dia*pers in.

dàizi is said with the fourth tone/falling tone. Since a bag is something into which you drop things, the falling tone seems appropriate.

袋 This character has the "clothing" radical 衣 on the bottom. A bag is a bit like a pocket in a garment, after all. The perfect phonetic on top is 代 , meaning "generation." It's composed of the "people" radical on the left and a spear or some such weapon on the right. Sadly enough, generation after generation of people have used weapons to kill their fellow human beings.

子 This character is a suffix that was added in the modern language and is a common ending on nouns.

dàlǐtáng 大禮堂/大礼堂 auditorium

"Hello, **Dolly**" is one of many musicals that might be performed in the *auditorium* of any **town**.

dà means "big" and is said with the fourth tone/falling tone, as befits a word with a strong meaning. *lǐ* means "rituals" and is said with the third tone/low rising tone, as seems appropriate since bowing low as a sign of respect is one of the major rituals of East Asia. *táng* means "large hall" and is said with the second tone/rising tone, since you generally must ascend the stairs in an auditorium to take your seat.

大 Usually pronounced as *dà*, as in the word for "big," you can remember this character by recalling that doctors are a big help in the fight against disease.

禮/礼 This character is written with the "God" radical 示 on the left, which shows something placed on an altar as a sacrifice to God. The "God" radical is often written on the left of a character, in which case it is distorted to look like a man in a necktie going to church. The right side of the traditional character shows two hands on top placing a 豆 radical, meaning ritual vessel, on the altar. The "mouth" radical here shows the mouth of the vessel, with the strokes below it indicating the base on which it stands. The simplified version of the character for "rituals" replaces the entire right side with a simple hook. Rituals serve as a spiritual hook, after all.

堂   This character means "large hall" and has the common phonetic 尚 on the top, showing the slanted roof tiles and roof of a Chinese home over a window, often seen in characters that end in the -ang sound. The radical is the "earth" or "ground" radical 土, indicating the clay or mud brick from which the walls of ancient halls were constructed.

dào   到   to arrive

*We investors always want to know what level the **Dow** has arrived at each day.*

Dào is said with the fourth tone/falling tone. It makes sense that the word "to arrive" would be said with a definitive intonation, as if to indicate success.

到   The left side of the character actually shows a bird dropping down from the sky and arriving on the "ground" radical 土. The right side is the "knife" phonetic 刀, which is always abbreviated like this when used on the right side of a character.

dàolǐ   道理   principle(s)

*We hope that **Dow** Chemical as well as **Dow** Jones will **duly** operate according to high-minded principles.*

A homonym with the **dào** that means "to arrive," the word for "principles" is also something that should be said with the decisive-sounding fourth tone/falling tone. **lǐ** is said with the third tone/low rising tone, as the principles by which you aim to lead your life gradually sink into your heart.

道　The character has the "foot" radical on the left and the character 首 meaning "head" or "principal" on the right. Although this character originally meant "road," a meaning it still retains, it also came to mean metaphorically the main path you take in life, i.e., the principles by which you live. By extension, it also came to mean the guiding principle of all life, a.k.a. Nature, a.k.a. "the Tao."

理　This character means "reason," as in the word "reasonable," as well as "principles." The character seems to have the king on the left. In the past people always naively hoped their king would rule by reason and by high principles. In truth the character has the "jade" radical on the left, 玉, which shows strings of jade on a necklace or bracelet. The metaphor is that, just as the pieces of jade are ordered when set in those pieces of jewelry, so should people's behavior be ordered by reason. The phonetic on the right, 里, is one of the most common phonetics in the Chinese language. The original meaning of the character 里, which it still retains, is a Chinese mile. It shows the measuring of the earth, 土, in a field 田.

děi　得　must; have to; got to

We __must__ be good to each other __day__ after __day__.

děi is said with the third tone/low rising tone. We don't always accept what we must do, and so perhaps that is why the word is said with a low dip to the voice in what seems grudging acceptance.

得　The character has the "double people" radical on the left, seeming to indicate the kindness with which we must treat our fellow human beings. On the bottom right is a "hand" radical 寸, above which is the character for "one," 一, on top of which is the "sun" radical 日. Think about the fact that with our actions, symbolized by the hand, each and every single day we _must_ be good to other people.

děng 等 to wait

*When you <u>wait</u>, be careful to not wait in the **dung**!*

děng is said with the third tone/low rising tone. As time weighs heavily on our hands when we wait, it seems appropriate that we dip low with our voice in the drawn-out third tone, with the intonation of grudging acceptance.

等 The character seems to show a double K-Mart sign, under which there seems to be a character, 土, that looks like a wrist watch over a character, 寸, that looks like a hand. Any of us who have shopped at a K-Mart know all about waiting in long lines to check-out, looking at our watch in impatience, as we say to ourselves "Oh, dung!" or words to that effect!

The true etymology has to do with the original meaning of the character, which is "rank" or "class," a meaning it still retains. The "bamboo" radical on the top symbolizes the bamboo slips officials at court would insert in the sash of their robes to indicate their rank. The "earth" radical 土 with the character for "inch," 寸, below it, which derives from a picture of the thumb and forefinger, represents the bequeathing of land by the king to his officials.

diǎn 點/点 a bit (of something); to light (a fire); to point

*It's every little <u>bit</u> of **DNA** we have that determines what each of us is like. Geneticists <u>point</u> to our **DNA** in explaining our physical makeup.*

diǎn is said with the third tone/low rising tone, as befits a word that means only "a little bit."

點/点 The traditional character has the character 黑, meaning "black," on the left side. The character for "black" shows a window blackened by soot from a fire, indicated by the "fire" radical 火 on the bottom, on a house made from mud brick, symbolized by the character for "earth" 土. The right side of 點 is a phonetic 占. That phonetic actually shows the cracks in a tortoise shell on top, with the mouth of a soothsayer on the bottom, and means "to foretell the future." The true etymology of this character has to do with the original meaning, which it still retains, of lighting a fire. By extension it came to mean the little bits that are left of whatever is burned by a fire. On top the simplified character looks a bit like a cigarette lighter being lit, as indicated by the "fire" radical below it.

diànnǎo   電腦/电脑   computer (literally: electric brain)

In our __dens__ most of us __now__ have <u>computers</u>.

diànnǎo is said with the fourth tone/falling tone followed by the third tone/low rising tone. When we type on the computer, our hands come down onto the keyboard from above, and then rise up again as we touch each key.

電/电   This character contains the "rain" radical 雨 on top, under which is a cloud with a tail of lightning coming out of it. The original meaning of the character was "lightning," from which people derived the idea of electricity. The character is now used as a common prefix for "electric." The simplified versions shows the cloud with the tail of lightning, looking a bit like Ben Franklin's kite being struck by lightning.

腦/脑   This is the character for "brain." It has the "flesh" radical on the left, with a picture of the brain on the bottom right, with what appear to be brain waves coming out on the top right. The simplified version appears to just show the brain marked by an X symbol enclosed in what seems to be the skull.

dìdi 弟弟 younger brother

*"**D, D** ..." represent the grades my <u>little brother</u> keeps getting in school!*

Dìdi is said with the fourth tone/falling tone. An older brother or sister might often use the commanding falling tone to order their little brother or sister to do something!

弟 The horns on top of the character symbolize power or authority. In traditional Chinese culture the younger brother, being a male, has some authority in the family. The rest of the character shows a thread, 弓, looking like the "bow" radical, being wound around a bobbin in a loom, represented by the vertical line. The metaphor here is that younger brothers, one after another, follow the birth of their older brother, just like threads follow one after another as the loom weaves.

dìfang 地方 place

*There are <u>places</u> that **de-fang** ferocious animals.*

dìfang is said with the fourth tone/falling tone. When you arrive at a place, you put your feet down and settle in, so the falling tone seems appropriate.

地 This character means "the earth" or "ground" and has the "earth" or "ground" radical 土 on the left, with the character 也, meaning "also," on the right. This could mean that, in addition to whatever <u>place</u> on the earth is being talked about, there are also many other <u>places</u> as well.

方 This character looks like a square boat lashed to the shore. Since the boat is tied to the shore at a certain <u>location or place</u>, it emphasizes the meaning of the compound word 地方.

dìlǐ 地理 geography

*Geography is a real **dilly** of a subject in school, encompassing so much about the topography of the earth as well as studying human activity.*

dìlǐ is said with the fourth tone/falling tone followed by the third tone/low rising tone. The intonation seems to follow the hills and valleys of the earth's terrain.

地   This character means "the earth" or "ground" and has the "earth" or "ground" radical 土 on the left, with the character 也, meaning "also," on the right. This could mean that, in addition to whatever *place* on the earth is being talked about, there are also many other *places* as well.

理   This character means "reason," as in the word "reasonable," as well as "principles." The character seems to have the king on the left. In the past people always naively hoped their king would rule by reason and by high principles. In truth the character has the "jade" radical on the left, 玉, which shows strings of jade on a necklace or bracelet. The metaphor is that, just as the pieces of jade are ordered when set in those pieces of jewelry, so should people's behavior be ordered by reason. The phonetic on the right, 里, is one of the most common phonetics the Chinese language. The original meaning of the character 里, which it still retains, is a Chinese mile. It shows the measuring of the earth, 土, in a field, 田.

dìng 訂/订 to reserve; to order

*When you wish to <u>reserve</u> a hotel room in person at the hotel, you often have to ring a bell (**ding, ding**) for service.*

dìng is said with the fourth tone/falling tone. When you order a book or reserve a hotel room you must do so with confidence and a commanding tone, so the decisive falling intonation seems appropriate.

訂/订   This character has the "speech" radical on the left, since before the days of computers you would usually order a book or reserve a hotel room verbally. The phonetic on the right is 丁, meaning "nail." When you make a reservation for a room, you want to _nail down_ that room by reserving it. The simplified version merely simplifies the "speech" radical on the left.

dìtú   地圖/地图   map(s)

Maps unfortunately do not show the **detours**.

dìtú is said with the fourth tone/falling tone following by the second tone/rising tone. When you look at a map you start by looking from top to bottom and then, most likely, back up again.

地   This character means "the earth" or "ground" and has the "earth" or "ground" radical 土 on the left, with the character 也, meaning "also," on the right. This could mean that, in addition to whatever _place_ on the earth is being talked about, there are also many other _places_ as well.

圖   The character 圖, in its traditional form, actually shows within the outer square a smaller square surrounded by a larger square on the bottom. These seem to represent a city's boundaries within the large boundaries of the district, with a dividing line above the two squares, which seems to indicate a border with another town to the north represented by the rectangle on top. The large square that encompasses all of the other strokes is the "enclosure" radical, here representing the map of the various towns.

图   The simplified form of the character ignores the etymology and replaces everything inside the map with the character 冬, which means "winter." Although this substitution seems completely arbitrary, it is true that it is in winter that a map is most crucial, since to be lost in winter while traveling might have dire consequences.

dìzhǐ　地址　address

*When UPS or FedEx deliver packages, they must look at their list of deliveries to find out which are the <u>addresses</u> "**du jour**."*

dìzhǐ is said with the fourth tone/falling tone, followed by the third tone/low rising tone, as is true of so many compound words in Chinese. As the deliveryman must travel downhill and then uphill to deliver packages to each address, so too does the voice in saying the word for "address" in Chinese.

地　This character means the earth or ground and has the "earth" or "ground" radical 土 on the left, with the character 也, meaning "also," on the right. This could mean that, in addition to whatever <u>place</u> on the earth is being talked about, there are also many other <u>places</u> as well.

址　This character has the "earth" or "ground" radical on the left side and is a perfect example of how the phonetic in a character so often contributes to the meaning. The phonetic character on the right side is 止, which means "to stop." Not only is it a perfect phonetic, but it emphasizes the meaning of the entire character 址, since when you arrive at the address you're seeking, you <u>stop</u> at that place on the <u>street</u>.

dōng　冬　winter

*Those of us who live in the north of the U.S. during a cold <u>winter</u> may say to ourselves "**Dang** winter!" or words to that effect.*

dōng means "winter." It is said with the first tone/high level tone, as is true of all the words for the four seasons of the year except for "summer." Think about the fact that, at least in northern climes, spring, fall, and winter seem long, drawn-out seasons, and therefore are appropriately said with the longer, drawn-out first tone. Summer, on the other hand, is said with the quicker falling tone, since its stay seems all too brief.

冬   The character for "winter" on top actually shows threads tied at the top of a loom, with the "ice" radical on the bottom. The metaphor here is that winter is the icy end of the year.

dǒng   懂   to understand

*"**Dong**!" It rings a bell for me! Now I <u>understand</u>!!*

dǒng is said with the third tone (low rising tone). When you understand something, we say in English that it "sinks in." Hence the low rising tone seems appropriate for the Chinese word.

懂   The true etymology of this character is simply that it has the "heart" radical on the left, since it is with the mind that we understand something. The phonetic on the right side, 董, is also pronounced *dǒng* and means "antique." It's composed of the "grass" radical on top with 重, meaning "heavy," as the phonetic on the bottom, which seems to show a bunch of weights piled up at the gym.

dōu   都   both; all

<u>All</u> of us need some <u>**dough**</u> to pay for the things we buy.

dōu is said with the first tone/high level tone. It somehow seems appropriate to elongate and thereby stress the word for "all" by saying it with the longer first tone.

都   A silly, but hopefully useful mnemonic device is to think about the fact that bakers, represented by what appears to be the letter B on the right of this character, work with dough, and must get up early, when the sun (日) is just beginning to appear over the earth (土). The truth is that the original reading of this character, which it still retains, was *dū* and means "capital city." That's why it has the "city wall" radical on the the right side, showing the building blocks of a city wall. The left side is a phonetic. The character was borrowed for its sound in devising a way to write the character for the spoken word that conveyed the abstract idea of "both; all."

duǎn 短 short (in length)

*Life is <u>short</u>, so it's all the more important to <u>**do on**</u> to others as you would have them <u>**do on**</u> to you.*

duǎn is said with the third tone/low rising tone. As you say the word, think of a short yoyo string, with the yoyo going down and then up.

短 This character has the "arrow" radical on the left side, with a character showing a ritual vessel, a pot or goblet, on the right. The actual etymology is that these were two relatively short objects in the ancient world.

duì 對/对 correct; right; to face

*Think of a person who's not particularly bright explaining to you how to do something and saying: "This is <u>**duh way**</u> to do it <u>right</u>."*

duì is said with the assertive fourth tone/falling tone.

對/对 The traditional character is based on the original meaning of "to face," which it still retains. It shows a hand on the right facing a thicket on the left, through which a person must pass. The simplified character shows two hands across from one another or facing one another. You can also think about the two hands applauding the right answer.

è 餓/饿 hungry

When we're really <u>hungry</u>, we may emit a sound very much like "<u>è</u>" (uh).

When we do express our hunger we might do so with a fourth tone/falling tone, similar to a sigh.

餓/饿 This character has the "food" radical on the left, which is made of a hand on top reaching in to a rice bowl in the middle and scooping up the rice with a spoon, shown on the bottom of the character. The phonetic on the right is 我. In the simplified character the "food" radical is a bare-bones outline of the traditional version, and is always simplified this way when on the left side of a character.

Éguó   俄國/俄国   Russia

When we think of <u>Russia</u> *invading the Ukraine, we say to ourselves* "<u>**Ugh! Guo**</u> *back to your own country!*"

Éguó is said with two second tones/rising tones in succession, as if asking "Russia?!"

俄   This character by itself originally had the meaning of "sudden." It has the people radical on the left. The phonetic on the right is 我, which is a fairly common phonetic in characters pronounced *e*. Obviously this was the original pronunciation of the character 我 when it was first used as a phonetic. The character 我 shows a "hand," 手, on the left holding a weapon called the "halberd," 戈, defending what is "mine." Many of us in the West look with dismay at Russia's use of military force, which may help you remember this character.

國   This character means "country" and is often seen as a suffix in the Chinese words for many countries in the world. The traditional character actually shows the borders of a country, symbolized by the large square, the "enclosure" radical. Within the boundaries of the country are a castle town, represented by the small 口, with the character 一 below it, perhaps representing a road, and with a halberd on the right. The idea is that the army of a country is to go on the roads to defend the cities of the country with their weapons.

国   The simplified character contains what appears to be the king within the boundaries of his country. It is actually the "jade" radical. The people of every nation tend to think of their nation as a precious jewel.

érzi 兒子/儿子 son

*Some parents, whose <u>sons</u> cause them aggravation, can be heard to exclaim, "**Aargh!**" And, of course, the <u>sons</u> of pirates can often be heard to exclaim, "**Rrrr!**"*

érzi is said with the second tone/rising tone, as if a parent is calling his or her son.

兒/儿　The traditional character shows a boy, with the head on top and two slits for the eyes, with two legs on the bottom. The simplified version only shows the legs.

子　This character is a suffix that was added in the modern language and is a common ending on nouns.

fàn 飯/饭 food; a meal

*I'm quite sure that like me, you are also a big **fan** of <u>food</u>. And it's a lot of **fun** to have a meal! Yes, the word is really pronounced like "fahn," but ...*

fàn is said with the fourth tone/falling tone. Since we put food down on the table when we are about to have a meal, the falling tone seeming appropriate.

飯/饭　This character has the "food" radical on the left. 反, which means "to turn over," is the phonetic on the right. It shows a hand (又), with palm down, being turned over, the motion of which is represented by the two-stroke character 厂. The phonetic slightly resembles a little tray table on which you might place a meal. The simplified character is exactly the same, except that the "food" radical on the left has been pared down.

fàng 放 to put/place

Vampires place their fangs into the throats of unwitting victims.

fàng is said with the fourth tone/falling tone. Since we speak of putting things down, the falling tone seems appropriate for a word that means to put something somewhere.

> 放 This character is written with two hands on the right, which also serve as the radical, placing something somewhere. The phonetic is 方, a common phonetic you can read more about under the entry for *dìfang*.

fēi 飛/飞 to fly

"Fay" is an old English word for "fairy," and fairies like Tinkerbell can certainly fly. The Chinese word sounds a bit like the English word "fly."

fēi is said with the first tone/high level tone, which allows it to be said with an elongated, floating sound.

> 飛/飞 The traditional character looks like a bird ascending to the sky (升) on its two wings (飞). While the character actually does contain the pictograph for wing doubled, combined with the character that means "to ascend" (升), the original pictograph actually portrayed the mythical phoenix in flight. The simplified character is just one wing.

fēicháng 非常 extraordinarily; extremely

Some movie stars are extremely fetching (fēicháng).

Fēicháng is said with the first tone/high level tone followed by the second tone/rising tone. When we say the word "extremely" in Chinese or English, we tend to emphasize the word by elongating it. Thus it seems to make sense that the Chinese word would begin with the first tone, since that is the most elongated of the four tones, with the voice rising up at the end with *cháng*.

非常 This character compound literally means "not ordinary," i.e., "extraordinary." 非 seems to show two hands in opposition, symbolizing "not ..." The character 常 has on the top the common phonetic 尚, showing the slanted roof tiles and roof of a Chinese home over a window, often seen in characters that end in the *-ang* sound.

The radical on the bottom is the "cloth" radical. The actual etymology is that a cloth flag was always held up at the head of an army. This character originally meant "always," but has come to mean "ordinarily," "ordinary," "usually," and "usual." Something that is "extraordinary" is "not ordinary" or "usual."

fēn 分 to divide; (a) penny; (a) minute

*You can have a lot of **fun** in one minute, as you can with a penny. And it's **fun** to divide things up and share them with our friends!*

fēn is said with the first tone/high level tone. As you divide things up, you extend them straight out to your family and friends, who are on the same equal plane with you.

分 The character has the "knife" 刀 radical on the bottom, with the two slanted lines above it indicating the cutting up and hence dividing of something. Used as a verb the word means "to divide." Since the smallest division of money is a penny and the smallest division of time, besides a second, is a minute, this character has come to mean both those things.

fùjìn 附近 vicinity; neighborhood; nearby

*Wherever we are, we want to know what's in the **fujinity** (vicinity).*

fùjìn is said with two consecutive fourth tones/falling tones. When something is in your neighborhood, you can drop in on that place very easily. The falling tone is said more quickly and is less elongated than the other three tones, so it seems fitting for words related to _short_ distances, i.e., nearby.

附 This character has the "city wall" radical on the left, with 付 as a perfect phonetic on the right. 附 by itself means "nearby area." The phonetic shows the "people" radical on the left with a hand extended on the right, paying money.

近 By itself this character means "close" or "near." It has the "foot" radical on the left, with an axe as the phonetic on the right, which also contributes to the meaning. The original idea was actually to get close enough on foot to your enemy to hew them with an axe.

_fù_   付   to pay

When we have to pay our bills, many of us say "Oh, **foo**!"

_fù_ is said with the fourth tone/falling tone, mimicking, perhaps, putting our money down on the table.

付 The character shows the "people" radical on the left with a hand extended on the right, paying money.

fùqin   父親/父亲   father

When we are children and ask our father for something, should he refuse, we say "Oh, **foo**!" In any case, we often look somewhat like him, and may even have his **chin**!

fùqin is said with the fourth tone/falling tone, the decisive commanding tone befitting a father's authority in the traditional Chinese family.

父 This character, which by itself means "father," shows the father's two hands raised above his head in a gesture of authority.

親/亲 This character was added as a suffix in the modern language to avoid confusion with other characters that are

homonyms. This character means "relative," so 父親/父亲
literally means "fatherly relative." The traditional form of
the character 親 has 見, meaning "to meet" or "to see," as the
radical, since relatives are people we see regularly in our lives.
The phonetic on the left has the character 立, meaning "to
stand," on the top, with the tree on the bottom. After all, relatives are people who "stand" in our family tree and whom we
see regularly. The simplified character eliminates the radical
and leaves only the phonetic part of the traditional character.

gānggāng 剛剛/刚刚 just a little while ago

*When a member of Jesse James's gang was caught and asked about
the whereabouts of Jesse and the boys, he said that the **gang** had
just left <u>a little while ago</u>.*

gānggāng is said with the first tone/high level tone. Just as
in English we tend to stress the word "just" in saying that
something just happened, the elongated high level tone for the
corresponding Chinese word allows it to be stressed in a similar
way.

剛/刚 The traditional character has the phonetic on the left,
which looks like the outline of a shack in which the "gang"
meets. Inside is the table where they sit. The "knife" radical is
on the right, the weapon of choice for this gang! In the simplified version, there is a simply an X in the shack, marking the
spot where the gang meets.

gāo 高 tall; high

*When a person is <u>tall</u> or a building <u>high</u>, our gaze will naturally **go**
upward.*

gāo is, of course, said with the first tone/high level tone, as befits
a word that means "high." It sounds like an aural description of a
high, level plateau.

高 This character is a picture of a two-story building, with
the roof on top and an upstairs and a downstairs window. In

ancient China, where most buildings were one story, any two-story building was considered tall.

gāoxìng 高興/高兴 happy (literally: "high spirits")

When you're in <u>high spirits</u>, you might feel like singing.

gāoxìng is said with a first tone/high level tone followed by a fourth tone/falling tone. You're in high spirits and then, with a falling tone, assert your happiness with the decisive fourth tone.

高 This character is a picture of a two-story building, with the roof on top and an upstairs and a downstairs window. In ancient China, where most buildings were one story, any two-story building was considered tall.

興 The traditional character 興 originally meant "spirits," as in "the spirits of the dead." On the top it shows two hands on either side, placing a ritual vessel on the altar (the bottom strokes) as an offering to the spirits of the ancestors. It is now used figuratively so that 高興 means "to be in high spirits," i.e., "happy" or "excited."

兴 The simplified version of the character only retains three slanted strokes on top, seen in so many simplified characters. Here they can be thought of as representing the spirits of the dead emanating down to us from the heavens.

gēge 哥哥 older brother

If your <u>older brother</u> likes men, or if he's just a really happy person, then you may think of him, lovingly, as "gay-gay"! O.K., O.K., the Chinese word is pronounced "guh-guh," but we're after a snappy mnemonic device here!

gēge is first tone/high level tone, a tone that befits his higher position in the traditional Chinese family hierarchy.

哥 This character shows two mouths with breath rising up from each. The actual etymology of this word is that it was originally the character for "song." It was pronounced exactly the same, which is why it shows multiple mouths singing together. The character 可 written twice also serves as a phonetic. Since the words for "older brother" and for "song" are homonyms, the character was borrowed for its sound. To avoid confusion, the character 歌 was created for "song," adding the "breath" radical on the right. To remember this character for "older brother," think about your older brother always mouthing off and telling you, his younger sibling, what to do. And perhaps your older brother likes to sing!

gěi 給/给 to give

To give to others is a gay and happy thing.

gěi is third tone/low rising tone. When people from East Asia give presents, they often bow low as they hand it to the recipient. Hence the low rising tone seems appropriate.

給/给 The left side looks like a Christmas tree, with the right side seeming to show a gift box (口) underneath the tree (top right part of the character). Of course the left side of the character is really the "silk" radical, with the right side showing perhaps a bolt of silk given by the emperor to his officials as part of their income. The simplified version has a slightly pared down "silk" radical.

gēn 跟 with; and; to follow

A policeman has a gun with/and a holster.

gēn is first tone/high level tone. When you do something with someone else, you presumably are on a level with her or him as social equals.

跟 The true etymology of this character has to do with the fact that its original meaning, which it still retains when used as a verb, is "to follow." Therefore it has the "foot" radical 足 on the left, with a fairly common phonetic on the right that is found in the following characters: 很, 恨, and 恳. The phonetic does look a bit like a person with head facing to the right and with the two legs on the bottom. It actually does show a person turning around suddenly, adding to the meaning of "to follow." By extension, as a helping verb it came to mean "with" as well as "and."

gōngkè 功課/功课 homework; school work

*Hopefully students are **gung**-ho about their classes (**ke**-lasses) and about their <u>school work</u>.*

gōngkè is said with the first tone/high level tone followed by the fourth tone/falling tone. Hopefully your homework is done on a high level, then dropped (respectfully) on the teacher's desk.

功 This character by itself means "achievement" or "merit." It has the carpenter's ruler on the left as the phonetic, with the "energy" radical on the right. A person can only achieve something through exerting a lot of energy. The carpenter's ruler contributes to the meaning, since it is related to the work of building something.

課/课 This character means "class" or "course." It has the "speech" radical on the left, with the character for "fruit" on the right, which looks like fruit growing on the top of a tree. To gain the fruits of knowledge, students must listen to the lectures of their teachers. The simplified version has a pared-down version of the "speech" radical.

gǒu 狗 dog

*When playing fetch with a <u>dog</u>, we throw a stick and say "**go** get it!"*

gǒu is said with the third tone/low rising tone. Dogs often lie down below their owners and then rise up when they hear a noise.

狗 The character has the "dog" radical on the left, with the curved vertical line representing the backbone of the dog and the two short skewed lines representing the front and back legs. Although the right side is a phonetic, it looks like a dog's owner is throwing a bone or stick (the outer strokes) while shouting, as represented by the "mouth" radical 口, to the dog to fetch it.

gòu (le) 夠/够 enough

After your dog has fetched a stick over and over, you say "__Go!__ That's __enough!__"

Gòu is said with the fourth tone/falling tone, which seems appropriate for a decisive word that declares you've had enough.

夠/够 The traditional character has the character for "many" or "a lot" on the left, showing two moons. You can think of the phrase "many moons ago." If you have a lot of something, you should realize you have enough. The phonetic on the right is the same one found in 狗, meaning "dog." The simplified version merely reverses the two sides of the character, which hardly seems a simplification!

guà 掛/挂 to hang

__Hang__ the __gua__va up to dry!

guà is said with the fourth tone/falling tone. In saying the word, the voice seems to mimic the action of hanging something up.

掛/挂 The traditional character has the "hand" radical on the left. In the middle, it seems pots are hung full of dirt (土). The two strokes on the far right seem to show a coat rack on which to hang coats. The simplified version omits the coat rack.

guài 怪 to blame; strange

Goo? Why is that strange? And why blame me?!

guài is said with the fourth tone/falling tone, an appropriately decisive intonation for a word that means "to blame."

怪 The character has the "heart" radical on the left. The right side shows a hand (又) over the place (土) where the heart is, expressing surprise at something strange.

guānxi 關係/关系 connection(s); relevance

Go on an' see what connections you can make with people of influence.

guānxi is said with the first tone/high level tone. When trying to establish connections with powerful people, you are always aiming at those in high positions. Hence the high level tone seems appropriate.

關 This character means "to close." It shows a doorway, in the middle of which are two locks (幺) above two bolts (丱). When you want to "close" a deal, you need to develop connections with that person, which often is done behind closed doors.

关 The simplified version of the character meaning "to close" seems to show a big, powerful person, with arms outstretched and horns to represent power, with whom you would like to develop connections and close the deal you have in mind.

係/系 This character has the "people" radical on the left, since people seek to make connections/relationships with other people. The meaningful phonetic, also pronounced *xì*, shows a single line above the "silk" radical and means "to tie." When we seek to make connections or develop relationships with other people, we attempt to tie them to us, figuratively speaking. The simplified version of the character simply omits the "people" radical.

guì 貴/贵 expensive

It's (G)Way too expensive!

guì is said with the fourth tone/falling tone, as you decisively state your opinion that something is pricey.

貴/贵 For both the traditional and simplified versions the top part shows a basket, and the bottom part has the "cowry shell" radical, which represents money. You needed a full basket of cowry shells to buy something expensive in ancient China.

guò 過/过 pass (by); go over; exceed

When you go (gwoh) by something, you have passed by it, or, metaphorically, exceeded it.

guò is said with the fourth tone/falling tone. When you pass by something, you glance at it quickly from top to bottom. And when you exceed something, you have metaphorically "topped" it. So the falling tone seems appropriate.

過 The traditional character has the "foot" radical on the left, indicating walking. The right side appears to be a two-story building, which you are *passing by* on foot. Actually the right side is the "bone" radical and serves as a phonetic.

过 In the simplified character, a "hand" radical replaces the phonetic on the right, so it seems you are waving as you "go (gwoh) by" someone or something on foot.

gùshi 故事 story

---

*Rich oilmen in Texas all have a <u>story</u> about their first **gusher**
(gu-sure).*

gùshi is said with the fourth tone/falling tone. After all, stories
are handed <u>down</u> from generation to generation.

故 The word for story possesses two hands on the right as
the radical, indicating something having been done. The phonetic on the left, 古, means "ancient," and contributes to the
meaning of "in the past." 古 is a combinational character, with
the "mouth" radical on the bottom and the character for "ten"
on the top. The idea truly was that, if something is ancient, it's
been passed down through ten generations by word of mouth.

事 This character means "occurrence" or "thing" and shows
a hand represented by the horizontal lines grasping a brush
and writing things down.

hái 還/还 still; in addition

---

*As impersonal as modern society may have become, we <u>still</u> say
"**hi**" to one another on the street.*

hái is said with the second tone/rising tone. When we pass
someone on the sidewalk, we raise up our hand in greeting as we
say "Hi!"

還 The traditional character has the "foot" radical on the
left. The phonetic on the right appears to show an eye on top,
below which is a mouth, with a hand waving at the very bottom. As you go by someone on foot, you see her or him, and
while saying "Hi!" you wave with your hand.

还 In the simplified version of the character, the phonetic is
replaced by the character 不, which looks like you are waving
hello with both hands.

hǎi 海 sea(s)

Adventurous people have always wanted to travel the **high** <u>seas</u>.

hǎi is said with the third tone/low rising tone. The sea is, after all, very deep, so the low tone seems most appropriate. Think, too, of a whale diving deep down into the sea and then coming up.

海 The character is written with the "water" radical on the left, as is true for all characters that describe bodies of water. The phonetic on the right, 每, means "every" and has the "people" radical on top and the character 母, meaning "mother," on the bottom. When we're confronted with a <u>sea</u> of troubles, <u>each</u> of us will want to turn to our <u>mother</u> for comfort.

háizi 孩子 child/children

When you see little <u>children</u>, you should always say "<u>Hi</u>!"
Although when I say that to one little shy <u>child</u> in our neighborhood, he always runs and **hides**!

háizi is said with the second tone/rising tone. Many parents of adult children, wanting grandchildren, will ask "Children?" with the rising intonation of a question.

孩 This character has the "child" radical on the left. It shows a baby in swaddling clothes, with the feet together and the arms sticking out. The pointed head at the top right of the radical indicates that the bones at the top of the baby's skull don't knit together until some time into the second week after birth. The phonetic shows a pig, turned 90 degrees to make it easier to write, with four legs on the left and the tail sticking out at the bottom right. This is a common phonetic in characters read *hai*, *gai*, etc.

子 This character is a suffix that was added in the modern language and is a common ending on nouns.

Hànyǔ 漢語/汉语 Chinese language

If you go to China and don't know <u>Chinese</u>, the joke's (h)<u>on you</u>!

hànyǔ is said with the fourth tone/falling tone followed by the third tone/low rising tone. As you start to say the word for the Chinese language, you begin with a confident falling tone, then, realizing how difficult it is to master the language, finish with a humble bow and a low rising third tone.

漢   The Chinese people have never called their country "China" or any word resembling it, nor have they ever referred to themselves by a word that sounds anything like "Chinese." Our terms in English come from the Qin dynasty, which only lasted around twelve years. It was not only short, but a very brutal period of time as well. The Chinese certainly don't want to be known as the people of "Qin," and prefer, instead, to call themselves people of "Han." The Han dynasty succeeded the Qin dynasty and was a golden age that lasted around four centuries. The dynasty took its name from the Han River, the area from which the family of the ruling dynasty came.

As a result the character 漢, pronounced *hàn*, has the "water" radical on the left. The right side of the traditional character is a phonetic, also found in the character 難, pronounced *nán*, which means "hard" or "difficult." It shows a cow's head on top, a distortion of a rice field (田) below that, with the character for "big" (大) on the bottom. The idea is that it is hard for the birds to survive when the fields turn the color of a cow's hide, i.e., brown.

汉   In the simplified character, the phonetic is replaced with a "hand" radical, palm down. Hopefully the <u>han</u>d will remind you of <u>Han</u>! And Chinese is the most commonly spoken language in the world, hands down, with nearly a billion speakers of Mandarin alone.

語/语   This character means "language." It logically has the "speech" radical on the left, which appears to have a mouth at the bottom with sound waves coming out of it. The original idea was actually breath or sounds emanating from the mouth. The right side of the character is a phonetic that somewhat contributes to the meaning. It is a classical word for "I." It contains the "mouth" radical on the bottom, with the character for the number 5, 五, on the top. Too much of human language consists of speaking about ourselves. In the simplified version of the character, the "speech" radical on the left is given in the skeletal outline generally used in simplified characters.

hǎo 好 good; fine; well; O.K.

*When asking others **how** they are, they almost always reply "good" or "fine" or "O.K.," regardless of how they're really doing.*

hǎo is said with the third tone/low rising tone. It seems fitting that the reassuring words "good" and "fine" are said with the comforting low tone.

好 The character shows a woman on the left with a child on the right. In traditional Chinese society, as in every traditional society, the highest good for a woman was to give birth to children so that they might carry on the family name.

hǎokàn 好看 good-looking; attractive

*To flatter someone on a date, it never hurts to ask: "**How can** you be so good-looking?!"*

hǎokàn is said with the third tone/low rising) followed by the fourth tone/falling tone. While **hǎo**, as mentioned above, is said with the comforting low tone, **kàn**, meaning "to look at," is said with the falling tone, since we tend to look people over from head to foot, i.e., with a falling gaze.

好 This character shows a woman on the left with a child on the right. In traditional Chinese society, as in every traditional society, the highest good for a woman was to give birth to children so that they might carry on the family name.

看   This character shows a hand on top shielding the eye, in order to see more clearly.

hē   喝   to drink

*hē is said with a slight throaty sound that almost mimics the drinking process. When we're served an alcoholic beverage that's new to us, after we <u>drink</u> it we may say "**Huh**?!"*

hē is said with the first tone/high level tone. After all, we raise a glass with any liquid on a <u>level</u> plane with our lips before we pour it straight back.

喝   This character has the "mouth" radical on the left, as you'd expect. The right side is a phonetic also used in 渴, the character for "thirsty." In both characters this phonetic contributes to the meaning. It shows a person (人) who is in wandering around lost, indicated by the lines surrounding the character for "person," and in need of some water to put in his mouth, with the top part of the character showing the mouth filled with something.

hēi   黑   black; dark

<u>Hey</u>, who turned out the lights! It's <u>dark</u> in here!

hēi is said with the first tone/high level tone, as if you're drawing out the English word "Hey!"

黑   The character for "black" shows a window blackened by soot from a fire, indicated by the "fire" radical on the bottom, on a house made from mud brick, symbolized by the character for "earth" 土.

hòu 後/后 behind; in back of ...

With a jolly "__ho__, ho, ho!" Santa Claus always has a sack of toys *__behind__ him, slung __in back of__ him.*

hòu is said with the fourth tone/falling tone. It's the intonation used by Santa when he says "Ho, ho, ho!" as well as the motion of him slinging his sack over his back.

後 The traditional character shows the "double people" radical on the left, appearing to depict one person behind another. It is actually a footprint. The right side shows two hands on the bottom dragging __behind__ a string or rope, represented by the "silk" radical on top.

后 The simplified version shows a mouth on the bottom __behind__ a hand that is covering it. It is traditionally the custom for Asian women to cover their mouths when smiling or laughing to avoid brazenly showing their teeth.

huā 花 flower

"__Hwaaah__," said slowly and elongating the "ah," is the sound of a *__flower__ opening.*

huā is first tone/high level tone. Think of a row of tall flowers, all the same height or level, to remember this is a first tone word.

花 The character has the "grass" radical on top. The phonetic on the bottom, 化, means to transform and contributes to the meaning. Flowers go through an amazing transformation, from their emergence from the ground to bud to bloom. The character 化 shows a person standing on the left and sitting on the right, changing position and thereby symbolizing transformation.

huá 滑 slippery; to slide

*When you are on a <u>slippery</u> sidewalk, you might say "<u>**Whaaat**</u>?!" with rising intonation. **huá** is actually a bit of onomatopoeia. It almost sounds like <u>sliding</u> when you say it.*

huá is said with the second tone/rising tone. When you slip and fall backward, your legs rise up in the air from under you. Saying this word with the rising tone gives you the sensation of slipping or sliding.

滑 This character has the "water" radical on the left, apropos of water on a road making it slippery. The "bone" radical on the right serves as the phonetic. The "bone" radical actually includes another radical, specifically the "flesh" radical 月 on the bottom. The idea is that flesh covers bone.

huà 畫/画 painting; picture

*Northern Chinese speakers will add an "r" ending and pronounce this word "huàr." Imagine an ill-educated American from the countryside coming into an art gallery and asking "<u>**Whar**</u> are the <u>paintings</u> at?"*

The word for *painting*, said with the fourth tone/falling tone, almost sounds like a painter taking a brush and running it down a canvas. And since Chinese paintings are scrolls that are hung from the top, the falling tone seems most appropriate.

畫/画 The traditional character shows a hand at the top holding a brush, represented by the long vertical line, and drawing a landscape, represented by the "field" radical 田 near the bottom. The very bottom stroke appears to be part of the picture frame. The simplified character has the "field" radical in the middle, with what appears to be a broken picture frame around it.

huàn 换 to exchange; change (money, clothes, etc.)

*Don **Juan** (pronounced "Huan" in Spanish) changed lovers every few days!*

huàn is said with the decisive-sounding fourth tone/falling tone. Like **huà**, the fact that the falling tone is the most abrupt of the three tones has the effect of the exchange or change being very sudden.

换 This character has the "hand" radical on the left, since we usually exchange or change money, clothes, etc. with our hands. The right side is the phonetic. It looks like it has a simplified picture of a hand on top, with the character 四, meaning "four," below it and the character for "big," 大, on the very bottom. Think about how you might exchange four coins, all quarters, for one big dollar bill.

huàxué 化學/化学 chemistry

huà *means to transform/change. It sounds like a magician removing the curtain in front of the box from which he has just made his assistant disappear.*

It's said with the fourth tone/falling tone. The falling tone is said more abruptly than the other three tones, and so has the effect of making the change seem very sudden.

化 The 化 character shows a person standing on the left and sitting on the right, changing position and thereby symbolizing transformation. Combined with the character 學/学 it produces, the Chinese term for "chemistry," literally "the study of changes and transformations."

學/学 The traditional version of this character shows two hands on either side of the top part, passing down knowledge to the student below, who is like a child (子) in his or her ignorance. The roof over the child's head seems to represent the confines of the student's mind. Studying will hopefully remove the roof, the barrier to learning, and allow true knowledge to enter. The simplified version reduces the entire top half of the character to three simple strokes.

huì 會/会 to know how to; can

If you can do something, you know the hway to do it.

huì is said with the fourth tone/falling tone, which is the decisive-sounding tone in Chinese. When you know how to do something, you're confident, and so the falling tone seems fitting.

> 會/会 The traditional character appears to be a bandit who has a hat on top, with a masked face underneath and a covered mouth on the bottom. This bandito certainly *knows how* to rob banks! The simplified character seems to show two noses under the roof. Two people *nose* (knows) better than one!

> The true etymology of the traditional character actually has to do with the original meaning of this word, which it still retains when used as a noun, namely "meeting." It shows the meeting in a doorway, under a roof, of several people, speaking together. The part on the very bottom, 曰, is not the "sun" radical, but rather depicts a mouth filled with words.

huíjiā 回家 return home

In hearing the nursery rhyme "Little Miss Muffet," in which she's eating her curds and whey, I asked "__Whey__? __Gee, ah__, what's that?!" We assume that Miss Muffet, after being chased away by a spider, presumably __returned home__ lickety-split!

huíjiā is said with the second tone/rising tone followed by the first tone/high level tone. Homes are ideally built on a high plane that is not subject to flooding, so it's appropriately said with the high level tone. When you return home, you then have to go uphill to arrive there, so the rising tone seems fitting.

回　This character means to return and originally was written as two concentric circles, representing the cyclical nature of returning. The two circles were later squared off, to make the character easier to write.

家　This character means "home" and shows a pig under a roof. The pig is turned 90 degrees to make it easier to write, with four legs on the left and the tail sticking out at the bottom right. The Chinese could never afford the wasteful practice of raising cows, which necessitates large tracts of land to graze, as their main source of meat. Country homes often had pigs sleeping with people under the same roof, albeit in a sty at the other end of the house from the family bedrooms.

huǒchē　火車/火车　train (literally: "fire vehicle," from the days of the steam locomotive)

If a fire breaks out, we say "__Whoa!__" Old cars will just __chug__ down the highway.

It's said with the third tone/low rising tone. Think of a fire pit, with the fire down at the bottom. *chē* is first tone/high level tone, as befits a vehicle that moves horizontally.

火　The character for "fire" shows flames lapping upward.

車/车　The traditional character actually depicts a cart, with the top and bottom horizontal strokes representing the wheels, the long vertical stroke showing the axle, and the middle section portraying the body of the cart, all from a bird's-eye view. The simplified character shows a bare-bones skeletal outline of the traditional character, which is how so many of the simplified characters were formed.

hùzhào 護照/护照 passport

We need to show our passport to officials at the airport, so they can know who Zhao is and who Zhou is.

hùzhào is said with two fourth tones/falling tones, as if customs officials are ordering you to hand over your passport with decisive falling intonation.

護 The traditional form of the character has the "speech" radical on the left, representing the use of a verbal arguments, perhaps in court, to protect or defend a person. The phonetic character on the right side has the "flower" radical on top, the "short-tailed bird" radical underneath it, and a "hand" radical on the bottom. Think about how important it is to act, symbolized by the hand, to protect the flowers and birds as humans continue to destroy their habitat.

护 The simplified character has the "hand" radical on the left, acting to protect something or someone, with 户, meaning doorway, as a perfect phonetic on the right. We must act to protect our homes, of course.

照 This character can be found in the Chinese word for photograph and by itself means "to shine" or "to illuminate." It has the "fire" radical on the bottom. The phonetic on top is composed of the "sun" radical on the top left, which contributes to the meaning of "to shine," and a "knife" radical above a mouth on the top right.

húzi 鬍子/胡子 beard

When someone whom you know but haven't seen for a long time reappears with a beard, you think to yourself "__Who's__ (huzi) behind that __beard__?!"

húzi is said with the second tone/rising tone, as if you're really asking "Who?" with the rising intonation of a question.

鬍/胡 The traditional character 鬍 contains the character 長, meaning long, on the top left, with long flowing hair on the top right. A beard is, after all, long flowing hair. The bottom of the character is the perfect phonetic 胡, meaning "barbarian." This is composed of the "moon" radical on the right side, symbolizing the barbarians living out in tents under the night sky. The phonetic for 胡 is the character 古, pronounced *gŭ*, which means ancient.

子　This character is a suffix that was added in the modern language and is a common ending on nouns.

Jī　雞/鸡　chicken

*Like the sound a <u>hen</u> makes on the farm—**"gee, gee, gee."***

jī is said with the first tone/high level tone. Think of a chicken sticking its neck straight out as it "gee, gee, gees."

雞　The traditional character has the "short-tailed bird" radical on the right. The phonetic on the left side shows on the top a hand reaching in for something, under which is the "silk" radical, with the character 大, meaning "big," on the very bottom. Imagine the "silk" radical as the chicken, with the farmer's hand reaching in to grab a large one for supper.

鸡　The simplified character on the right has the "long-tailed bird" radical in its simplified form. On the left is simply a hand that appears to be grabbing the bird.

jiālĭ　家裏/家里　at home; in the family

*Hopefully everything <u>at home</u> and <u>in the family</u> is **jolly**.*

jiālĭ is said with the first tone/high level tone, followed by the third tone/low rising tone. *jiā* means "home" or "family," so think about the high roof of your home. *lĭ* means "inside," so the low tone seems appropriate, as if you're diving down inside some safe place.

家　This character means "home" and shows a pig under a roof. The pig is turned 90 degrees to make it easier to write, with four legs on the left and the tail sticking out at the bottom right. The Chinese could never afford the wasteful practice of raising cows, which necessitates large tracts of land to graze, as their main source of meat. Country homes often had pigs sleeping with people under the same roof, albeit in a sty at the other end of the house from the family bedrooms.

裏/里   The traditional version of this character has the "clothing" radical (衣) split with the phonetic 里. The original idea really was something "inside" a garment. The phonetic 里, meaning "mile," combines the "field" radical on the top with the character for "earth" or "ground" on the bottom. The idea was actually to measure the land in the fields in _miles_. The simplified character just uses the phonetic.

jiàn   見/见   to meet

*When you _meet_ people these days, they're usually wearing **jean**s (jee-ens)!*

jiàn is said with the fourth tone/falling tone. When you meet people, you tend to look them up and down, from top to bottom, so the falling tone seems fitting.

見/见   The traditional character shows the "eye" radical 目 on top of two legs, both things you use when you meet or see someone. The simplified character pushes the two legs up into the head, which has got to hurt!

jiāo   教   to teach

*"**Gee, 'ow** I love _to teach_," my Cockney friend said to me.*

jiāo is said with the first tone/high level tone. Teachers should live up to _high_ standards as a model to their students and should always _level_ with them.

教   The character has two hands on the right, symbolizing the passing of knowledge from teacher to students. The phonetic on the left, 孝, meaning "filial piety," is significant. This virtue was one of the first things taught in Chinese schools in the past. It shows the old, represented by an abbreviated form of the character 老, taking precedence over the young (子).

jiào 叫 to call; to tell (someone to do something)

"Hey, Joe (gee-ow)!," you might hear someone call out.

jiào is said with the fourth tone/falling tone, since when you call out to someone, it's with a quick, decisive, falling intonation.

叫 The character has the "mouth" radical on the left, with what appears to be the Arabic numeral 4 on the right. It's as if you're asking "What are you calling me *for* (*four*)?!" The true explanation of the character is that the right side is a plant extending out its tendrils. When we call out to someone, we are using our mouth to send out a call, just as the plant sends out its shoots.

Jīdūtú 基督徒 Christian

When you say the Chinese word for "Christian," it sounds like you're saying "God, the Holy Spirit, and Jesus, too."

jīdū, which actually means "Christ," is said with two first tones/ high level tones. Christ calls us to a high level of conduct, of course. *tú* means disciple. It is said with the second tone/ rising tone, as if the disciple is trying to rise to the high level of conduct set by Jesus.

基 This character means "foundation" or "base." Christ is the foundation of a Christian's faith. The "earth" radical is on the bottom of the character, indicating what a "foundation" is built on. 其 looks like a wheelbarrow, with the two long vertical lines as the handles and the two little lines on the bottom as the wheels. When building the foundation of a building, you need to use a wheelbarrow to haul the bricks.

督 This character means "to oversee." God oversees all human activity. The character has the "eye" radical on the bottom. The phonetic on top, 尗, shows a hand on the right picking beans from the plant on the left. Perhaps this is a good metaphor for Christ picking his disciples?

徒　This character means "follower." It has the "double person" radical on the left, which is actually a footprint. The disciple follows in the footsteps of his master. The right side is the character 走, which means "to go." It shows the foot in motion on the bottom, with the sole and heel of the foot raised, walking along the ground.

jiē　接　to receive; to pick (someone) up (at the airport, etc.)

When we need someone to <u>pick</u> us <u>up</u> at the airport, train station, at school, etc., we might say "__Gee, uh__ ... could you pick me up?" And they might say "Gee, ah ... I'd like to, but ..."

jiē is said with the first tone/high level tone. When you go to greet the person whom you've arranged to pick up, you make a beeline straight to them. The high level tone seems appropriate in expressing that.

接　The character shows the "hand" radical on the left. This character can mean to receive a thing as well as to greet a person. In either case, we use our hands one way or another. The phonetic on the right, 妾, means "concubine." Although the true etymology of 妾 is a woman whose hair is piled high on her head, it appears to be a combination of the character 立, showing a person standing and 女, the character for "woman." Think of a female relative or friend standing somewhere waiting for you to pick them up and give them a helping hand.

jiè　借　to lend; to borrow

When we're strapped for cash, we might say "__Gee, uh__ ... could I <u>borrow</u> some money."

jiè is said with the fourth tone/falling tone. This word can mean either "to borrow" or "to lend", depending on whether you put 跟 + somebody in front of it or 给 right after it. The falling tone seems particularly apropos when *jiè* means "to lend," as the lender drops the loaned object into the palm of the borrower.

借 The character has the "people" radical on the left. It is only people who lend or borrow things. Animals just take what they want without asking. The right side of the character appears to have a shorthand version of the number 21, written in Chinese as 二十一, on top, with the character for "sun" or "day," 日, on the bottom. 21 days is exactly the period of time that we can <u>borrow</u> books from the library.

jiějie 姐姐 older sister

My <u>older sister</u>, Jenny, is always asking our parents: "**Gee uh**, may I borrow the car?"

jiějie is said with the third tone/low rising tone. Younger brothers and sisters should bow low and lower their voices to their older sisters out of respect. At least that's what MY older sister tells me!

姐 This character has the "woman" radical on the left. Not surprisingly, the terms for all female family members in Chinese contain the "woman" radical, usually on the left but occasionally on the bottom of the character. The phonetic on the right seems to show a mirror, into which big sister is looking and saying "Gee, uh, aren't I pretty?"

jièshao 介紹/介绍 to introduce

"**Gee, uh, show** me that person and <u>introduce</u> us!"
(Last time I use "gee, uh" as a mnemonic device, I promise!)

jièshào is said with the fourth tone/falling tone. When you introduce yourself, you must do so with confidence. The falling tone is the confident, decisive-sounding tone in Chinese.

介 This character depicts two people being introduced to one another under a roof.

紹/绍 This character was added in the modern language to avoid confusion with other homonyms. It has the "silk" radical on the left, with the phonetic 召 on the right. When you're introduced to someone you might put on a silk shirt or blouse and invite them to have a meal with you. During the course of the meal you cut the meat or bread for them with a knife (刀) and let them partake (口).

jīn 金 gold

*When a **gen**ie (from the Arabic word "jinn") grants a wish in the Arabian nights, most people ask for gold.*

jīn is said with the first tone/high level tone. Tall piles of gold, stacked evenly, are stored in Fort Knox.

金 This character has the "earth" radical on the bottom, with the two short skewed lines on either side of it being nuggets of gold in the earth. The top lines show the gold buried under the ground.

jìn 近 near; close

*A bartender will keep his **gin** near him at all times, in order to make gin and tonics.*

jìn is said with the fourth tone/falling tone. The fourth tone is the quickest and shortest of the four tones, and thus seems fitting for a word that means "close."

近 This character has the "foot" radical on the left and an "axe" on the right . The true etymology is to get near enough to the enemy to strike him with your axe. Such was ancient Chinese warfare. The axe is also a phonetic. The brilliance of the Chinese written language includes the fact that the phonetics so often contribute to the meaning of characters.

jīngjì 經濟/经济 economy

*The economy for us personally is all about the **jingle** of coins in our pocket, metaphorically speaking.*

jīngjì is said with the first tone/high level tone followed by the fourth tone/falling tone. It seems that whenever the economy reaches a new high, it inevitably then falls.

經/经 This character means "to pass through" or " to manage." It has the "silk" radical on the left. The silkworm cocoons have to pass through many stages before being woven into silk. In the top of the phonetic on the right side water is shown coursing through an underground passage. Both the radical and phonetic are done in skeletal form in the simplified version.

濟/济 This character means "to aid," but its etymology has to do with its original meaning of "crossing a river." As a result it has the "water" radical on the left, with a phonetic on the right that means "symmetric." To those of us who are Christians, it might look a bit like the Y in Christ on the cross, with the two thieves on either side of him, and a ladder on the bottom that the soldiers used. In the simplified version, the phonetic is a bare skeletal outline of the original phonetic.

jìnlái 進來/进来 to come in; to enter

*Many a falsehood is said under the influence of alcohol. Should a lover of gin and tonics come into a bar and make a bogus boast, you could call that a "**gin lie.**"*

jìnlái is said with the fourth tone/falling tone followed by the second tone/rising tone, in roller coaster fashion, as if the roller coaster is *entering* into a dive and then *coming* up again.

進/进 The traditional version of this character has the "foot" radical on the left and the "short-tailed bird" radical on the right. By itself, this character means "to enter" and depicts a bird hopping in on foot. The simplified character replaces the bird with a phonetic, using the character 井, which means "water" or "well." We might approach a well on foot and drop a penny *in* it!

來/来   The character 來 means "to come." It contains the "tree" radical, which also represents large plants, such as wheat or rice plants. What looks like two small "people" radicals (人) actually represents ears of grain. The original idea was that this character represented the arrival of harvest time. The China of two to three millennia ago, which produced the characters still used today, was an agricultural society. So for the people of that time, most of whom were peasants, the metaphors they used often had to do with planting and harvesting. The simplified character reduces the two ears of grain to two grains.

jiǔ   酒   alcohol

*My buddy, **Joe**, drives an old **Geo** and drinks a lot of* *alcohol.*

jiǔ is said with the third tone/low rising tone. When we drink alcohol, or any beverage, we pour it *down* into our throats.

酒   This character has the "water" radical on the left, since alcohol is a liquid. The phonetic on the right side contributes to the meaning by showing a bottle with a stopper on it at the top. The small horizontal line near the bottom of the bottle indicates the level of the remaining alcohol.

júzi   橘子/桔子   oranges (the tangerine oranges we call "Mandarin oranges")

*Oranges are wonderfully **juicy**. (Your mouth should water as you say this!)*

júzi is said with the second tone/rising tone. Think of the juice squirting up into your face.

橘   This character has the "tree" radical on the left, as with all the characters for fruits that grow on trees. The complex phonetic on the right seems to show a child on the top, standing on a crate that has oranges inside it. Of course this is just a fanciful mnemonic. The child is actually the character for "spear," and the orange is the "mouth" radical.

桔 The simplified character uses the character 吉, meaning "good fortune," as a simpler phonetic. It depicts a scholar representing a fortuneteller on top, predicting good fortune for the listener.

子 This character is a suffix that was added in the modern language and is a common ending on nouns.

kāishǐ 開始/开始 to begin

*"Let's <u>begin</u>, o**kay**?" "**Sure**, we can <u>begin</u>."*

kāishǐ is said with the first tone/high level tone followed by the third tone/low rising tone. So often we begin an endeavor with a high level of expectations, only to have to lower them afterward.

開/开 This character means "to open." It depicts the "door" radical 門 with two hands, represented by the two small vertical lines, taking the bolts from the door, which are represented by the two small horizontal lines. The simplified version of the character just shows the hands removing the bolts from the door as if to open it.

始 This character means "beginning." We all begin life inside a woman (女), our mothers, as a little nose and mouth.

kàn 看 to look at; to see; to watch

*Most of us take for granted the blessing that we **can** (kahn) look at things and see them.*

Kàn is said with the fourth tone/falling tone. When we look at things, we tend to let our gaze fall over something, looking from the top to the bottom.

看 The character actually shows a hand on top shielding the eye (目) in order to see better.

kǎo 烤 to grill; to roast; to bake

*In summer we often grill **cow** meat, which we call "beef."*

kǎo is said with the third tone/low rising tone. We lower the beef onto the grill, after all.

烤 The character has the "fire" radical on the left. The phonetic on the right side looks very much like the character 老, meaning "old." 考 has the "earth" radical on the top. On the bottom of the character it appears smoke is rising up from the ground where someone is grilling meat.

kǎoshì 考試/考试 a test; to take a test

*Students often see tests as a bunch of **cow shi-**. **Sure** they do!*

kǎoshì is said with the third tone/low rising tone followed by the fourth tone/falling tone. When said quickly, it almost sounds like a sneeze! It does seem some students are allergic to tests!!

考 This character is the phonetic for the character 烤, which means to grill. When teachers give difficult tests to students, they are said to be "grilling" their students.

試/试 This character means "to try" or "to try out (something)." Tests are to try out or test your ability at a subject. The character has the "speech" radical on the left, since often tests are given orally. The perfect phonetic on the right shows a carpenter's ruler on the bottom left (工) with a dart or small arrow on the right. The character 式 means "style," with the metaphor being that weapons are made in a certain style or form according to certain measurements, or the carpenter's ruler. Every test is given in a certain style or manner, after all.

kě 渴 thirsty

*When you're kě, you want to **hē** ("drink"), asking "**ken**" ("can") I have a can of something to drink? I'm thirsty!"*

kě is third tone/low rising tone. When you're thirsty, you want to pour something liquid down into the bottom of your throat.

渴 The character has the "water" radical on the left, since when you're thirsty, you're in search of water or anything liquid. The phonetic on the right side is the same phonetic used in the character 喝, meaning "to drink." In both characters this phonetic contributes to the meaning. It shows a person (人) wandering around lost, indicated by the lines surrounding the character for "person," and in need of some water to put in his mouth. The top part of the character shows the mouth filled with water.

kè 課/课 class; course

*I never **cut** my **ke**-lasses (classes)!*

kè is said with the fourth tone/falling tone. Something so critical to a student should be said with the decisive- and affirmative-sounding falling tone, as when we say "*YES*, I *WILL* study for my classes!"

課/课 The character has the "speech" radical on the left, since so much of class in school involves speaking. The phonetic on the right side means "fruit." It seems to show a fruit tree on the bottom growing in a field, located at the top of the character. The true etymology is that the "field" radical on top originally showed a fruit on the tree. If the classes you choose are well taught, you will gain the "fruits" of knowledge.

kèqi 客氣/客气 polite

*It's not <u>polite</u> to go up to an adult and say "**koochie, koochie, koo!**" (Or, in the Chinese case, "**kuhchee, kuhchee, kuu!**")*

Kèqi is said with the fourth tone/falling tone). A polite person in East Asia lowers or drops the head in bowing to someone they meet.

客   This character means "guest." It has the "roof" radical on the top. The phonetic below it, 各, meaning "individual," shows two legs at the top and the "mouth" radical on the bottom. It contributes to the meaning of the entire character, since the actual etymology was to go your own way without heeding the advice of others, and thus needing shelter as a guest in your travels.

氣/气   This character means "air." It depicts how air rises up from the bottom right to the top left. In the traditional character, the character for rice, 米, is used simply as a phonetic. When you cook rice, steam will rise up! The simplified version of the character omits the phonetic. This is a common way to simplify many of the Chinese characters.

kū 哭 to cry

*When we're sad, we often "**ku**-ry" (<u>cry</u>).*

kū is said with the first tone/high level tone. The first tone is the longest, most drawn-out of the tones. When you say *kū*, it's as if you're giving a long, drawn-out sob.

哭   The character show a dog on the bottom (犬), always turned 90 degrees from the original drawing to make it easier to write, with two mouths on top. The actual etymology was a dog howling, in its intensity sounding like two people crying.

kuài 快 fast; quick; soon

The Bridge over the River Kuai had to be built quickly (do you know that Academy Award-winning movie?) I want to visit the Hawaiian island of Kauai soon!

kuài is said with the fourth tone/falling tone. Since the falling tone is said the most abrupt and quickest of the four tones in Chinese, it seems appropriate that it be used for a word that means "fast."

快 Both of the characters for "fast" and "slow" (慢) have the "heart" radical on the left, representing the heart beating fast or slowly. The phonetic on the right side of 快 shows a person running along with arms akimbo. It reinforces the idea of the heart beating rapidly when a person is running.

là 辣 spicy; hot

"Ou la la, that's spicy!" said the French chef on tasting Sichuan dishes with the black peppers.

là is said with the fourth tone/falling tone, appropriately decisive- and strong-sounding for a word denoting a strong, decisive flavor.

辣 The character seems to show a large plant on the right, represented by the "tree" radical, with a large hot pepper growing on it. The left side looks a bit like a person, with the long, curved vertical line representing the legs in a leaning position, overcome by the extreme spiciness of the dish she/he just ate.

lái 來/来 to come

*Don't **lie** to me! Are you <u>coming</u> to the meeting or not?!*

lái is said with the second tone/rising tone, as if you're coming up the stairs.

> 來/来 This character means "to come." It contains the "tree" radical, which also represents large plants, such as wheat or rice plants. What looks like two small "people" radicals (人) actually represents ears of grain. The original idea was that this character represented the arrival of harvest time. The China of two to three millennia ago, which produced the characters still used today, was an agricultural society. So for the people of that time, most of whom were peasants, the metaphors they used often had to do with planting and harvesting. The simplified character reduces the two ears of grain to two grains.

lǎo 老 old (for people and animals)

*We should al-**low** <u>old</u> people to take our seats on the bus.*

lǎo is said with the third tone/low rising tone. Old people need to sit down more than young people.

> 老 Usually when 土 appears at the top of a character, rather than meaning "earth" it instead depicts the head of a person. The true etymology of this character supposedly is that it shows the head of an old man with the beard trailing off his chin to the right. It looks more like the bent leg of an old person on the bottom, with the long curved line in the middle representing a cane, by which the old person supports herself/himself while walking along the ground (土).

lǎoshī 老師/老师 teacher

Most <u>teachers</u> are not a **louse**. A respectful student al**<u>lows her</u>** to share her knowledge with the class.

lǎoshī is said with the third tone/low rising tone followed by the first tone/high level tone. Asian students bow low to the teacher and then bring their body back to the level position.

老 See the entry for *lǎo*.

師/师 This character originally meant the general in an army who protects the city walls. Therefore the left side shows the building blocks of a city wall, while the right side contains the "cloth" radical (巾), representing the flag flying above the city ramparts. In time it came to be someone in charge of anything, i.e., a "master." The true etymology aside, the left side looks like the head of a teacher with a cowlick along with his belly, while the right side seems like a teacher standing rigidly in front of a class. The simplified form on the left seems to show a very slender teacher in profile, while the right side has the teacher facing the class with arms held down at her/his side.

lèi 累 tired

I was <u>tired</u> and so **lay** down.

lèi is said with the fourth tone/falling tone. When you lay down, you dropped onto the bed or sofa.

累 The character has the "field" radical on top and the "silk" radical on the bottom. It's tiring work raising silkworms in the fields! The actual etymology has nothing to do with the idea of "tired," since this character was borrowed simply for its sound. The original character had three fields on top as a phonetic. The "silk" radical on the bottom represents the original idea of "involved" by the metaphor of things being tied together, poetically speaking.

lěng 冷 cold

*When it's <u>cold</u>, it gets you in the **lung**s.*

lěng is said with the third tone/low rising tone. In English we talk about the cold settling or sinking in.

冷 The character has the "ice" radical on the left, representing the idea of "cold." The right side shows an office of an official below a roof-like structure, and means "command." Although just a phonetic, it does look a bit like a person standing under a roof and taking shelter from the cold.

liǎn 臉/脸 face

*Nothing is sweeter than when someone you love **leans** their <u>face</u> against yours.*

liǎn is said with the third tone/low rising tone, as if you are leaning your face down onto your pillow.

臉 The character has the "flesh" radical on the left, which is the radical for all fleshy body parts in Chinese characters. The phonetic on the right side of the traditional character certainly looks like a carved pumpkin face, with two eyes and two teeth under the lid of the carved pumpkin.

脸 The simplified version eliminates the eyes and has three jagged teeth in the mouth, represented by the three skewed lines between the two horizontal ones.

lǐbài 禮拜/礼拜 worship; week (traditional word for xīngqī)

It's not appropriate to go to <u>worship</u> in <u>Levi</u>'s. But the tribe of <u>Levi</u> in ancient Israel were those who oversaw <u>worship</u> in the temple.

lǐbài is said with the third tone/low rising tone followed by the fourth tone/falling tone. In worship, you bow your head in prayer, then nod in agreement with the minister's sermon.

禮/礼 This character means "ritual." It has the "God" radical on the left. The phonetic on the right side contributes to the meaning. It shows two hands at the top placing a ritual vessel (豆) on an altar. The simplified character replaces the meaningful phonetic with a hook. Ritual is the ceremonial hook that brings us closer to God.

拜 This character means "pay respects to" or "to show obeisance." It depicts two hands pressed together in worship.

lìshǐ 歷史/历史 history

---

*<u>History</u> is written about the **lìshǐ** (leader) of a country.*

lìshǐ said with the fourth tone/falling tone followed by the third tone/low rising tone. Histories are usually written from the top of the society down to the bottom, i.e., from kings to peasants.

歷/历 This character depicts history marching on. The traditional character has the "foot" radical on the bottom. Near the top, under the roof and side wall of a storage place, are two "grain" radicals. To the largely agricultural society of ancient China, history was a procession of harvests each year. The simplified character replaces the two grain plants with the "energy" radical as a phonetic, as if symbolizing all the energy human beings have expended throughout our history.

史 This character shows a messenger carrying a package or message to deliver, with the bottom two strokes representing the legs. History has messages to bring us about the past, to help us better manage the future, if we would but listen.

lǐtou   裏頭/里头   inside; in

---

*In **Lido** Beach (Sarasota, Florida) there's a lot of sand. And, after being on Lido Beach, there's a lot of sand <u>inside</u> our **Le**vi's and <u>in</u> our <u>toes</u>!*

lǐtou is said with the third tone/low rising tone, as if you're digging your toes deep down into the sand.

裏/里   The traditional version of this character has the "clothing" radical (衣) split with the phonetic 里. The original idea really was something "inside" a garment. The phonetic 里, meaning "mile," combines the "field" radical on the top with the character for "earth" or "ground" on the bottom. The idea was actually to measure the land in the fields in <u>miles</u>. The simplified character for "inside" just uses the phonetic.

頭/头   The traditional form of the character shows the head on the right side, with 目 representing the face, wrinkle lines and all; the top of the skull is shown on top and the two lines on the bottom represent a beard. The phonetic on the left means "beans." The true etymology of the phonetic has to do with the fact that it shows a ritual vessel, with the 口 representing the mouth of the bowl or goblet. The simplified character seems to show a person (大) standing there with the two small lines on the top left pointing to the person's head.

lóu   樓/楼   floor (of a building); multi-storied building

---

*I live on a **low**er <u>floor</u> of the <u>building</u>.*

lóu is said with the second tone/rising tone, as if you're walking up the stairs to a higher floor in a building.

樓   The character has the "tree" radical on the left, since most buildings in ancient China were made of wood. The phonetic on the right side of the traditional character contributes to the meaning by showing a two-story, i.e., multi-storied building, in which the wives (女) of the emperor were housed.

COMMON CHINESE WORDS / 89

楼　The simplified character substitutes 米 (rice) for the two stories of the building, keeping the woman on the bottom. Presumably the women living in that building made dinner with rice.

lù　路　road

*On the <u>road</u> I'll skip to my **Lou**.*

lù is said with the fourth tone/falling tone, mimicking your footfall on the road.

路　The character has the "foot" radical on the left. The phonetic on the right has two legs on the top right and a mouth on the bottom. It contributes to the meaning by showing someone setting off on foot down the road for a journey without heeding the advice or words of others.

lǜshī　律師/律师　lawyer

<u>Losers</u> in lawsuits against employers need better <u>lawyers</u>.

lǜshī is said with the fourth tone/falling tone followed by the first tone/high level tone. The law comes *down* heavily on offenders, but ideally dispenses a *high level* of justice.

律/律　This character means "law." It has the "double people" radical on the left. Laws govern the relationships between people, after all. The right side of the character shows a hand holding a writing brush and writing down the judgment of the court.

師/师　This character originally meant the general who protects the city walls. Therefore the left side shows the building blocks of a city wall, while the right side contains the "cloth" radical (巾), representing the flag flying above the city ramparts. In time it came to be someone in charge of anything, i.e., a "master." The true etymology aside, the left side looks like the head of a teacher with a cowlick along with his belly, while the right side seems like a teacher standing rigidly in front of a class. The simplified form on the left seems to show a very slender teacher in profile, while the right side has the teacher facing the class with arms held down at her/his side.

lǚxíng 旅行 to travel

When you <u>travel</u>, you're **loosening** your ties with the place you're leaving.

lǚxíng is said with the third tone/low rising tone followed by the second tone/rising tone. It's as if you're traveling from a valley up into the mountains.

旅　This character seems to show a person (top right) traveling in different directions (bottom right) and going from place to place (方). Some etymologists believe that方 derives from the Buddhist "swastika" symbol, which shows that God is everywhere—north, south, east, west, up, and down, i.e., everywhere. Chinese books about etymology maintain that the left side and top right side of the character 旅 represent the overhanging branches of a tree, under which a traveler takes refuge.

行　The original meaning of this character is "to go." The two sides of the character actually show two footprints, but it looks like the intersection of two streets.

mǎ 馬/马 horse; a common surname

A cowboy might say "that's **ma horse**"!

mǎ is said with the third tone/low rising tone. After all, we sit down on the horse, so the low tone makes good horse sense.

馬/马　The traditional character shows the head and flowing mane of the horse on the top half of the character, with the four legs at the bottom. The simplified version gives a bare bones outline of the original character.

mà 罵/骂 yell at; scold; curse

---

*My **ma** would often yell at me, usually with good reason!*

mà is said in the decisive and curt fourth tone/falling tone.

罵/骂 The top part of the character shows two mouths. When someone yells at or scolds you, it sounds like two people shouting at you. The horse on the bottom is a phonetic. Of course, when you are thrown off a wild horse, there is some yelling and cursing that goes on!

máfán 麻煩/麻烦 trouble; bother (both a noun and verb)

---

*A **muffin** is a lot of trouble to make, which is why we love the Muffin Man!*

máfán is said with two second tones/rising tones, like muffins rising in the oven.

麻 This character means "marijuana" or "hemp." When you possess marijuana illegally, you do get in a lot of trouble! The character actually shows two trees, representing large hemp plants, being dried under the roof and sidewall of a shed.

煩/烦 This character has the "fire" radical on the left and the "head" radical on the right. Fire to the head is certainly a serious trouble!

mǎi 買/买 to buy

---

*When you buy Oscar **Mayer** cold cuts and look at the price these days, you exclaim "**My**, oh **my**!"*

mǎi is said with the third tone/low rising tone, as you dig deep down into your pocket for your wallet to buy things.

買 The traditional character actually shows a net on the top of the character, with the "cowry shell" radical symbolizing money on the bottom. In ancient China, cowry shells were used as currency. When you went to buy something, you would have to scoop up a bunch of cowry shells to go make a purchase.

买   The simplified version shows a person with two lines on the top left seeming to point to the head, and with a roof above. It appears this person has lost their head over some purchase in a store that they couldn't really afford!

mài   賣/卖   to sell

My, oh my, do I want to sell MY car and be done with all these repairs!

mài is said with the decisive-sounding fourth tone/falling tone, as opposed to *mǎi*, said with the much more submissive-sounding third tone.

賣/卖   The traditional character adds a 士 (person) on top of 買 (to buy), to emphasize the person *selling*, and hence meaning "to sell." The simplified form abbreviates the person on top of the character "to buy" to only two strokes (十).

māo   貓/猫   cat

The meow of the cat has inspired many languages to use an onomatopoeic word for that furry pet, including in ancient Egyptian.

māo is said with the first tone/high level tone. This seems most appropriate, since cats are usually found sleeping in the prone position in high-level places, such as our sofas and beds!

貓   The traditional character has the "cat" radical on the left, showing a front paw raised over the head, with the four legs and curved backbone of the cat below. The phonetic on the right, 苗, meaning "sprouts," has the "grass" radical on the top and the "field" radical on the bottom. Cats are just little sprouts that do enjoy chewing on tender grass shoots in our gardens to clean out the fur balls in their stomachs.

猫   The simplified character substitutes the "dog" radical on the left for the "cat" radical, an indignity for which cats will find it hard to forgive the Chinese! To be fair, however, the "dog" radical is the radical for the great majority of Chinese characters representing animals. It shows the curved backbone of the dog with the slanted horizontal lines representing the front and back legs.

màozi   帽子   hat; cap

*The Cat (**māo**) in the <u>Hat</u> (**màozi**)!*

màozi is said with the fourth tone/falling tone. After all, our hat comes down over our head.

帽   This character has the "cloth" radical on the left, referring to hats being originally made of some kind of cloth material. The perfect phonetic on the right shows the sun on top and the eye below it, as if the cloth hat is shielding the eyes from the sun.

子   This character is a suffix that was added in the modern language and is a common ending on nouns.

měi   美   beautiful

*The month of **May** is <u>beautiful</u> in most places in the U.S.*

měi is said with the third tone/low rising tone. The third tone is a rather comforting sound and is used for a number of Chinese words with very positive and affirming meanings.

美   This character has a sheep on top (羊) and the character 大 , meaning "big," on the bottom. While a large sheep is certainly a beautiful sight to a sheep farmer, providing him with lots of wool and mutton, the real etymology is much more interesting and profound.

The character 大 originally meant "person," with the horizontal line showing the outstretched arms of a person, with two legs on the bottom. The metaphor was that a person was considered "beautiful" if they were meek, mild, and humble, like a sheep. The classical Chinese word for "goodness" (善) , as well as the character for "righteousness" (義), also contains the character for sheep. In time the word 美 evolved from meaning internal beauty to the more superficial meaning of outward beauty.

Měiguó　美國/美国　America

After a while in China, most Americans say "__May__ I __go__ home to Meiguo?"

Měiguó is said with the third tone/low rising tone followed by the second tone/rising tone. In saying the word, it seems the Chinese are mirroring America's rise to superpower status.

美　These characters literally mean "beautiful country." The name in Chinese for America actually derives from the way the Chinese created names for many Western nations. As a rule, they took the first syllable of that country's name in the language of that country and chose a character with a positive meaning that was close to that sound. Since there is no Chinese word pronounced *a*, except for the exclamation 啊, the Chinese focused on the second syllable of aMErica and chose a word that meant "beautiful."

國　This character means "country" and is often seen as a suffix in the Chinese words for many countries in the world. The traditional character actually shows the borders of a country, symbolized by the large square, the "enclosure" radical. Within the boundaries of the country are a castle town, represented by the small 口, with the character 一 below it, perhaps representing a road, and with a halberd on the right. The idea is that the army of a country is to go on the roads to defend the cities of the country with their weapons.

国　The simplified character contains what appears to be the king within the boundaries of his country. It is actually the "jade" radical. The people of every nation tend to think of their nation as a precious jewel.

mèimei 妹妹 younger sister

*Little sisters are always saying "**May** I have this?" or "**May** I have that?"*

mèimei is said with the fourth tone/falling tone, as if you're the older sister or brother ordering your little sister around with the commanding sound of the falling tone.

妹妹 Like almost all the characters for female relatives in Chinese, the radical is the "woman" radical. And, like almost all informal and affectionate names for family members, the word is repeated. The phonetic on the right of 妹 shows a tree on which the top branches haven't yet grown out. Younger sisters are like trees that haven't fully developed.

měitiān 每天 every day

May tea an' biscuits be something you enjoy every day, like the British do!

měitiān is said with the third tone/low rising tone followed by the first tone. **měi**, meaning "every," has to be the low tone, weighed down by the weight of *every*thing! **tiān**, meaning "day," literally means "sky" or "heaven," which is the space above our heads.

每 This character contains the "person" character (人) on top and the "mother" character (母). 母 shows a mother's two breasts, turned 90 degrees to make it easier to write. Since *every* person has a mother, the phonetic contributes to the meaning.

天 This character shows a person (大) under the sky (一). Since we know the change of the days by the change of light in the sky, 天 has come to mean "day" as well as "sky."

méiyǒu   没有   not have; there isn't/aren't ...

---

*There isn't any **mayo** in traditional Chinese cooking, so the Chinese don't have **mayo** in the kitchen.*

méiyǒu is said with the second tone/rising tone followed by the third tone/low rising tone. As you finish the mayo in the jar, your spoon goes down into the bottom of the jar.

没   This character has the "water" radical on the left with two hands on the right, pushing something down under the water until it's no longer there. This is one of a handful of characters used for negation, with this character reserved to negate action verbs in the past. It is also used for negation in the past, present, and future when used with the verb 有, meaning "to have."

有   This character shows a hand (the top two strokes) holding what appears to be the moon, but is actually a piece of meat. It is a distortion of the character 肉. For Chinese peasants, especially in past centuries, meat was an extremely rare treat. Hence the word "to have" shows the hand holding something special, i.e., a piece of meat.

mén   門/门   door; gate

---

*If you have a lot of **mon**ey, you better keep your door locked!*

mén is said with the second tone/rising tone, as if you're lifting up the door handle to open it.

門/门   The traditional character shows the two leaves of the traditional Chinese door or gate. Although the pictograph resembles doors in a saloon in the old West, the traditional Chinese door extended all the way to the ground. The simplified character is a skeletal outline of the original.

COMMON CHINESE WORDS / 97

mìshū 秘書/秘书 secretary

In past generations, a low-class British boss could say to his <u>secretary</u>: *"This is* **me shoe**. *Go polish it!" Hopefully those days are gone for good!*

mìshū is said with the fourth tone/falling tone followed by the first tone/high level tone. It's as if the secretary is putting down or letting fall various papers onto a high, level desk.

秘 Meaning "secret," this character has the "grain" radical on the left, indicating a secret store of grain someone is keeping for themselves. The right side is a phonetic. It resembles a group of bees in a hive in a hidden or secret place. The right side is actually the character 必, meaning "must." It really shows a target pierced in the middle by an arrow, which the archer <u>must</u> do in order to win the archery contest.

書/书 This character means "book." It shows a hand on the top holding a writing brush represented by the vertical line, with the bristles pressed down flat on the paper, writing down something that you want to say. Those words are represented by the mouth on the bottom of the character, with the horizontal line in the box representing the mouth filled with speech.

mǔqīn 母親/母亲 mother

"Moo" goes the <u>mother</u> *cow. And our* **chin** *often resembles that of our mother.*

mǔqīn is said with the third tone/low rising tone followed by the first tone. The third tone has the comforting intonation you'd expect for the word for "mother."

母 Meaning "mother," this character shows a mother's two breasts, turned 90 degrees to make it easier to write. The breasts refer to the mother nursing an infant.

親/亲 This character was added as a suffix in the modern language to avoid confusion with other characters that are homonyms. This character means "relative," so 母親/母亲 literally means "motherly relative." The traditional form of the character 親 has 見, meaning "to meet" or "to see" as the radical, since relatives are people we see regularly in our lives. The phonetic on the left has the character 立, meaning "to stand," on the top, with the tree on the bottom. After all, relatives are people who "stand" in our family tree and whom we see regularly. The simplified character eliminates the radical and leaves only the phonetic part of the traditional character

nǎinai 奶奶 paternal grandmother

*No need to worry, little one. Your "nainai" is **nigh** (near).*

nǎinai is said with the third tone/low rising tone, which is the most comforting in feeling of the four tones in Chinese.

奶奶 This character has the "woman" radical on the left, which is true of almost every Chinese character for female family members. And, like the words for almost every family member in Chinese, the character is said twice. The right side shows a woman's breast.

nǎlǐ, nǎlǐ 哪裏, 哪裏/哪里, 哪里 not at all (traditional humble response to a compliment, literally meaning "where, where [do you get that]?")

*When people compliment Chinese people, it gets pretty **gnarly** when it comes to a response, given the emphasis on humility in Chinese culture.*

nǎlǐ, nǎlǐ is said with two third tones/low rising tones. It seems an appropriately humble intonation to lower your voice down to the bottom of your range, as if bowing vocally.

哪 This character means "which" and has the small "mouth" radical on the left, with the phonetic 那 on the right.

裏/里 The traditional version of this character has the "clothing" radical (衣) split with the phonetic 里. The original idea really was something "inside" a garment. The phonetic 里, meaning "mile," combines the "field" radical on the top with the character for "earth" or "ground" on the bottom. The idea was actually to measure the land in the fields in _miles_. The simplified character for "inside" just uses the phonetic.

nán 難/难 difficult; hard

Naan (India's special bread) is _difficult_ to make.

nán is said with the second tone/rising tone, as if asking if something is difficult by saying "hard?" with the rising intonation of a question.

難/难 The right side of the character is the "short-tailed bird" radical. The left side of the traditional character is a phonetic, also found in the character 漢/汉, meaning "Chinese." It shows a cow's head on top, a distortion of a rice field (田) below that, with the character 大 ("big") on the bottom. The idea is that it is hard for the birds to survive when the fields turn the color of a cow's hide, i.e., brown. The simplified character substitutes a hand, palm down, for the phonetic. It is very difficult to catch a bird with your hand!

náqǐlái 拿起來/拿起来 to pick up (an object)

To pick up **_nachos_** that are **_lying_** there on the table is irresistible!

náqǐlái is said with the second tone/rising tone followed by the third tone/low rising tone. The rising intonation of the word mimics the action of picking something _up_.

拿/拿 This character has the "hand" radical at the bottom seeming to grab a nacho or a Nabisco cookie (口) from under the lid of a cookie jar.

起 This character means "to rise up." It has the character 走, meaning "to go," on the left, which shows a character that looks like a foot on the bottom (止), with the heel and sole of the foot raised, walking along the ground (土). The phonetic on the right, pronounced *jǐ*, looks like a silk worm crawling upward.

來/来 This character means "to come." It contains the "tree" radical, which also represents large plants, such as wheat or rice plants. What looks like two small "people" radicals (人) actually represents ears of grain. The original idea was that this character represented the arrival of harvest time. The China of two to three millennia ago, which produced the characters still used today, was an agricultural society. So for the people of that time, most of whom were peasants, the metaphors they used often had to do with planting and harvesting. The simplified character reduces the two ears of grain to two grains.

néng 能 able to; can

néng sounds a bit like a bear growling. The bear is physically <u>able</u> to do just about anything it wants!

néng is said with the second tone/rising tone, adding to the feeling that it's a bear bellowing.

能 The character actually depicts a bear, with the head and body on the left side of the character and the two front paws with claws raised on the right. Chinese texts on the character's etymology explain that a bear is physically capable of doing almost anything, hence the meaning of the character.

nèr/nàr 那兒/那儿 there

"It's <u>there</u>, you **nerd**!"

nèr/nàr is said with the decisive-sounding fourth tone/falling tone, as if you're saying "There!" very emphatically.

那/那 This character means "that." The character actually has the "city wall" radical on the right side, with a fur coat pictured on the left side. It was the name of a city in the northwest of China, where the inhabitants wore fur coats in winter, due to the cold climate.

兒/儿 This character is a common suffix added to many nouns in northern speech. In this case it changes "this" to "this place," i.e., "here."

nǐ 你 you (singular)

*You little guy, who only comes up to my **knee**.*

nǐ is said with the third tone/low rising tone, with the voice lowering in pitch as if falling down to knee level.

你 The character has the "people" radical on the left. The right side has a roof on top with the side eaves, and the character 小, meaning "little," below it, as if the Chinese really were saying, "You little guy who only comes up to my knee!"

nián 年 year

*On the outside of some businesses, the **year** they started may be shown by a **neon** sign.*

nián is said with the second tone/rising tone, as if you were being questioned as to the *year* of your birth.

年 The character combines in condensed form the character 千, meaning "thousand," with the "grain" radical 禾. The ancient Chinese thought of each passing year as another harvest of thousands of wheat and rice plants.

niànshū 念書/念书 to study

*Many children need a **knee in** their back, figuratively speaking, to get them to study, since they're always saying "shoo!" when it comes to the books they're supposed to read.*

niàn is said with the fourth tone (falling tone), as if indicating the student's head dropping down over the book before them. The word **shū** for "book" is said with the first tone (high level tone), as if indicating books lying flat down on a high table.

念 This character has the "heart" radical on the bottom and the character 今 , meaning "now," on the top. Since the "heart" also symbolizes the mind in Chinese characters, the idea was actually that when you study, you should have your mind on the present moment.

書/书 This character means "book." It shows a hand on the top holding a writing brush represented by the vertical line, with the bristles pressed down flat on the paper, writing down something that you want to say. Those words are represented by the mouth on the bottom of the character, with the horizontal line in the box representing the mouth filled with speech.

niú 牛 cow(s)

When said in long, drawn-out fashion, it does sound somewhat like a <u>cow</u> bellowing.

niú is said with the second tone/rising tone, which helps to create the onomatopoetic sound of a bellowing cow.

牛 The character shows a bird's-eye view of a cow. The two horizontal lines represent the front and back legs of the cow, with the slanted line at the top left indicating a horn.

nǚ 女 female

*Too many <u>females</u> end up saying, "I **knew** (knee-yew) it. I **knew** you wouldn't marry me!"*

nǚ is said with the third tone/low rising tone. The submissive low tone of Chinese reflects the low position of women in Chinese society in the past.

女 The character shows the crossed arms and legs of a woman bowing, symbolizing the duty of women to yield to men in traditional Chinese culture.

COMMON CHINESE WORDS / 103

Ōuzhōu 歐洲／欧洲 Europe

One thing the U.S. has that Europe *hasn't got—*HoJo's *(Howard Johnson's)! "*Oh, Joe!*The Euro zone is in economic trouble? Say it isn't so, Joe!"*

Ōuzhōu is said with two first tones/high level tones. You might expect level, flat tones for a continent that isn't anywhere as mountainous as the western United States—except for Switzerland, of course!

歐／欧   This character has three little boxes on the left, which appear to represent three great European cities like London, Paris, and Rome, all enclosed within the European continent. The right side actually does show a person on the bottom with breath coming out, represented by the two lines on the top. It's as if tourists from other parts of the world are sighing in amazement at the historical sites in beautiful European cities. The simplified version substitutes an X for the three boxes on the left side of the character. The real etymology of this character is that the left side is a perfect phonetic. The right side was added just to create a character to represent "Europe" by transliterating the first syllable of the word in some Western languages.

洲   This character means "continent." It has the "water" radical on the left, since continents are generally separated from one another by large bodies of water. The perfect phonetic on the right originally meant "administrative district" and is now used as the suffix for the names of "states" or "provinces." It shows three small strokes representing pieces of land separated from each other by the three longer vertical strokes representing bodies of water. 川, meaning "river," shows water flowing downstream in a river bed. If states or provinces are spits of land separated from each other by rivers or smaller bodies of water, continents are larger pieces of land separated from each other by much larger bodies of water, i.e., oceans.

pà　怕　to fear; be afraid of

*My **Pa** is afraid of my Ma!*

pà is said with the fourth tone/falling tone. The abrupt, decisive-sounding falling tone seems appropriate for expressing a sudden jolt of fear.

怕　The character has the "heart" radical on the left, with the character 白, meaning "white," on the right side. When we feel fear in our hearts, our faces turn pale with fright. Although the character 白 is pronounced *bái* in modern Chinese, and the character 怕 is now pronounced *pà* , around 1,800 years ago, when the phonetics were created, both were most likely pronounced as *bo*. 白 was intended as a phonetic that contributed to the meaning.

pàng　胖　fat

*When you say this word with an explosive "p" sound, your cheeks will puff out and get **fat**. **Fat** people tend to get hunger **pangs** far too often!*

pàng is said with the fourth tone/falling tone, as if your doctor is pronouncing you "fat" with a decisive, commanding tone of voice.

胖　The character has the "flesh" radical on the left, looking exactly like the character for "moon." On the right side is the character 半, meaning "half," which was meant as the phonetic. It shows a cow (牛) being butchered in half, with the two short skewed lines at the top indicating that the cow has been cut in half. Of course if you eat a half of a cow in one sitting, you will get fat!

pánzi   盤子/盘子   plate(s)

---

*Our kitchens are full of <u>plates</u> and **pans**.*

pánzi is said with the second tone/rising tone, as if you're lifting up a plate to rinse it.

盤/盘   The traditional version of this character has the "plate" radical on the bottom, resembling a butter dish. The phonetic on top, meaning "ordinary" or "common," shows a boat on the top left, with the stern rudder on the top, with the gunnel represented by the horizontal line, and the people in bow and stern represented by the two very short strokes. On the right side of the phonetic are two hands using poles to move the boat along the river, which was a common way to steer a boat in China for many centuries. In the simplified character, the phonetic is reduced to just the "boat" radical.

子   This character is a suffix that was added in the modern language and is a common ending on nouns.

pǎo   跑   to run

"<u>Pow</u>!" There's the gun and the sprinters start to <u>run</u>.

pǎo is said with the third tone/low rising tone, as if one runner slipped and fell down.

跑   The character has the "foot" radical on the left, and the phonetic character 包 on the right, resembling a runner curled up on the ground under a shelter at the end of a long race.

The "foot" radical 足 includes another radical that means "foot," 止, on the bottom. The longer vertical line in 止 represents the ankle, the shorter vertical line the heel. The line on the bottom of the sole of the foot and the shorter horizontal line seem to represent the big toe. The little square on top of 足 can be imagined as the kneecap, although in the original pictograph it just shows the contours of the foot.

The phonetic 包 means "to wrap" and actually shows a person with their arms wrapped around some large object.

piányi 便宜 inexpensive; cheap

At **Penney's** most things are quite <u>inexpensive</u>. Even the **peons** find their clothing quite cheap.

piányi is said with the second tone/rising tone, as if expressing surprise or delight at how cheap something is.

便宜 The character 便 has the "people" radical on the left, with what appears to be a "peon" on the right, with a hat on top and two legs on the bottom, marching toward the right into a J.C. Penney's to shop. The character 宜 seems to show a small step ladder under the roof of a store, which is a rather inexpensive item. Since these characters were simply borrowed for their sound to match the pronunciation of the word for "inexpensive," the true etymology will not help us remember the characters.

píjiǔ 啤酒 beer

If you drink a lot of <u>beer</u>, it does make you **pee**! Just ask my buddy, **Joe!**

píjiǔ is said with the second tone/rising tone followed by the third tone/low rising tone, as if the beer were gradually going down your throat and settling to the bottom of your stomach.

啤 This character has the "mouth" radical on the left. The phonetic on the right looks like a person standing. The lower horizontal line represents the arms and hands, with one finger on the bottom left raised to the lips to remove the beer foam from his lips. This character is simply a transliteration of the first syllable of "beer" in English.

酒 This character means "alcohol." It has the "water" radical on the left, since alcohol is a liquid. The phonetic on the right side contributes to the meaning by showing a bottle with a stopper at the top. The small horizontal line near the bottom of the bottle seems to indicate the level of remaining alcohol.

píngzi 瓶子 bottle(s)

<u>Bottles</u> will "**ping**" *if you strike them just right with your index finger.*

píngzi is said with the second tone/rising tone, as if you're lifting a bottle of soda pop to your lips.

瓶 This character is written with the little-used "tile" radical on the right, which depicts a roof tile. Bottles in ancient China were made from the same clay material as were the tiles on roofs. The phonetic for 瓶 is 并, which depicts two people standing side by side with the intention of " lining up." People who love to drink will often line up their empty bottles on the table in the bar.

子 This character is a suffix that was added in the modern language and is a common ending on nouns.

qián 錢/钱 money

I have a <u>**yen**</u> *for* **qián** *(<u>money</u>).*

qián is said with the second tone/rising tone, as if soliciting funds by asking, "Money?" with a questioning intonation.

錢/钱 The character has the "gold," as in metal, radical on the left, which refers to metal coins. The phonetic on the right in the traditional character shows two halberds, i.e., two weapons to protect the gold. The simplified character gives a skeletal outline of both the radical and the phonetic.

qiántóu   前頭/前头   in front

*When walking down the street, you should keep your **qián** (money) in front of you, and not in your back pocket.*

qián, like the word *qián* for money, is said with the second tone/ rising tone.

> 前   The top of the character 前 seems to show the two feet of a thief, who creeps into a bank or house at night under the moon (月) while holding a knife, represented by the character on the bottom right. The original pictograph actually showed a boat (舟) in front of the shore. The two strokes to the right of it depict waves, and the two strokes on top of the character show grass growing along the shore.

> 頭/头   The traditional form of the character shows the head on the right side, with 目 representing the face, wrinkle lines and all; the top of the skull is shown on top and the two lines on the bottom represent a beard. The phonetic on the left means "beans." The true etymology of the phonetic has to do with the fact that it shows a ritual vessel, with the 口 representing the mouth of the bowl or goblet. The simplified character seems to show a person (大) standing with the two small lines on the top left pointing to the person's head.

qìchē   汽車/汽车   automobile; car

Cheech and ***Chong*** *(1970s and 1980s comedy duo) loved riding around in their car together.*

qìchē is said with the fourth tone/falling tone followed by the first tone/high level tone. On a convertible, when it rains you lower the top down, then drive straight ahead.

> 汽   This character has the "water" radical on the left, with the right side representing water rising up from bottom right to top left as it evaporates into the air. 汽 means "steam" and refers to the steam rising from the radiators of the early automobiles.

車/车   The traditional character actually shows a cart, with the top and bottom horizontal strokes representing the wheels, the long vertical stroke showing the axle, and the middle section portraying the body of the cart, all from a bird's-eye view. The simplified character shows a bare-bones skeletal outline of the traditional character, which is how so many of the simplified characters were formed.

qǐlái   起來/起来   to get up; arise

*When your room is **chilly**, it's hard <u>to get up</u> and out of bed in the morning.*

qǐlái is said with the third tone/low rising tone followed by the second tone/rising tone. The rising intonation of the word reflects the physical action of rising up.

起   The character means "to rise up." It has the character 走, meaning "to go," on the left, which shows a character that looks like a foot on the bottom (止), with the heel and sole of the foot raised, walking along the ground (土). The phonetic, on the right, looks like a silk worm crawling upward.

來/来   This character means "to come." It contains the "tree" radical, which also represents large plants, such as wheat or rice plants. What looks like two small "people" radicals (人) actually represents ears of grain. The original idea was that this character represented the arrival of harvest time. The China of two to three millennia ago, which produced the characters still used today, was an agricultural society. So for the people of that time, most of whom were peasants, the metaphors they used often had to do with planting and harvesting. The simplified character reduces the two ears of grain to two grains.

qīnqì 親戚/亲戚 relative(s); relation(s)

*The **chinchilla** is a <u>relative</u> of the mink.*

qīnqì is said with the first tone/high level tone followed by the fourth tone/falling tone. As you grow up, first you become the same height as many of your relatives, and the next thing you know, you're looking at them from above and you look down sort of like the fourth tone/falling tone looks down.

親/亲 This character by itself means "relative." The traditional form of the character 親 contains 見, meaning "to meet" or "to see" as the radical, since relatives are people we see regularly in our lives. The phonetic on the left has the character 立, meaning "to stand," on the top, with the tree on the bottom. Relatives are people who "stand" in our family tree and whom we see regularly. The simplified character for "relative," 亲, eliminates the radical and leaves only the phonetic.

戚 This character also means "relative" or "relation." It seems to show our desire to protect our relatives, who are part of our family tree or plant (朿) and we shelter under our roof (厂) and defend with weapons (戈) if necessary.

qítā 其他 another; additional

*The **cheetah** is <u>another</u> big cat, in addition to the lion and tiger.*

qítā is said with the second tone/rising tone followed by the first tone (high level tone), as if the cheetah is jumping up to a high level place.

其 The character means "that" or "it." It seems to show a little robot on two short legs as it moves to fulfil its function.

他 Although this character now means "he" or "his," the original meaning was "other." It has the "people" radical on the left and the character for "also" on the right. The idea was that it would refer to oneself, but also the other person or people to whom one was speaking.

qù 去 to go

*Ah-**choo** (chee-yew!)*

When this word, said with the fourth tone/falling tone, is pronounced decisively, it sounds very much like a sneeze. "**Go** blow (your nose)!"

去 The character seems to show the nose of a dog on the bottom going along the ground (土) and sniffing. The original pictograph actually showed the lid of a pot being taken off, hence the idea of "going away" and, by extension, "to go."

ràng 讓/让 to allow; to let; to have someone do something

*The Hunchback of Notre Dame **rang** (rahng) the church bells because the priest <u>allowed</u> him to do so.*

ràng is said with the fourth tone/falling tone, which intonation seems appropriate for a higher-up giving permission to an underling.

讓/让 This character has the "speech" radical on the left, since giving someone to do something is often done verbally. The phonetic on the right side in the traditional character shows the "clothing" radical (衣) split into two sections, with the two pockets of a knapsack constituting the middle. The simplified character swaps the simple character 上 for the phonetic.

rì 日 day

*We human beings **err** every <u>day</u> in some way or other.*

rì is said with the fourth tone/falling tone, as daylight falls on the earth at the break of day.

日 The character was originally a circle with a dot in the middle, indicating the sun, the rising and setting of which divides day from night.

Rìběn 日本 Japan

*Japan is largely an **urban** country.*

Rìběn is said with the fourth tone/falling tone followed by the third tone/low rising tone. Japan's economy fell after World War II, only to rise up again in the 1960s and 1970s.

日本   The country's name literally means "sun's origin" and is written the same way in Japanese. The rising sun is shown on the national flag. The name actually refers to the fact that Japan is to the east of China, and east is where the sun rises or "originates." The origin of the name was a letter written around 1,500 years ago by the ruler of Japan to the emperor of China. It began by saying "the ruler where the sun originates (日本) greets the emperor where the sun sets."

róngyi 容易 easy

*A ladder with **rung**s is <u>easy</u> to climb.*

róngyi is said with the second tone/rising tone, and sounds like you're tossing off the word with great ease.

容   This character looks like a Mexican bandito with sombrero, under which are two eyes, a mustache, and a mouth. The true etymology is that the character means "to encompass" or "to contain." It shows a roof on top that encompasses a house. The four slanted lines under the roof represent the folds of a mountain that encompass a valley below, represented by the square at the bottom.

易   This character may be seen as the bandito's trusty little pony. It's easy for this bandito to get money, because he simply steals it from banks (Politically incorrect mnemonic devices are often the most memorable, I'm afraid!). The character 易 means "change." It shows a chameleon, with the head and four legs. A chameleon easily changes its color.

ròu 肉 meat

Rover loves meat!

ròu is said with the fourth tone/falling tone, as if dropping a piece of meat down on the cutting board before carving it up.

肉 The character shows a piece of meat, with the two 人 radicals showing the marbling of the fat in the meat.

sànbù 散步 to take a walk

When Brazilians take a walk, they might samba a little.

sànbù is said with two fourth tones/falling tones, like feet coming down on the pavement as you walk.

散 This character means "to scatter." It shows two hands on the right as the radical. The phonetic on the left seems to show little bits of grass on the top with the moon on the bottom. At night little creatures like rabbits scatter about to eat whatever grass they might find.

步 This character means "steps." It shows the foot at rest on the top (止), with the sole and heel of the foot flat. On the bottom the foot is depicted in motion, with the sole and heel of the foot raised as if in midstep.

sǎodì 掃地/扫地 to sweep the floor

In **Saudi** Arabia with all that sand they have to sweep the floor a lot!

sǎodì is said with the third tone/low rising tone followed by the fourth tone/falling tone. When you sweep, first the broom is lowered to the floor, then raised again to sweep again.

掃/扫 This character by itself means "to sweep." It has the "hand" radical on the left side. The right side shows a hand on top holding a duster, represented by the "cloth" radical (巾) under the roof of a house. The simplified character reduces the right side to just a hand.

地　This character means "ground" or "floor" and has the "earth" or "dirt" radical on the left. The right side is the character 也, meaning "also," which seems to indicate the idea of "and also *this place* on the ground."

sēnlín　森林　forest; jungle

*There is little **sun in** the <u>forest</u> or <u>jungle</u>, due to all the trees.*

sēnlín is said with the first tone/high level tone, followed by the second tone/rising tone. Out of the high, even canopy of trees in the forest or jungle a bird suddenly rises up in flight.

森林　The first character shows three trees and the second character shows two trees. When a symbol like the "tree" radical is doubled in a Chinese character, it means that there is a lot of whatever that character represents. Three of anything means a really huge number of that thing. Of course there are huge numbers of trees in a forest or jungle.

shā　殺/杀　to kill

*The **Shah** of Iran <u>killed</u> many people during his reign. His secret police **shot** and <u>killed</u> many men.*

shā is said with the first tone/high level tone, as if shooting someone with a straight shot.

殺/杀　The traditional character shows on the left a dagger, represented by an X, made of wood (木). The right side of the character has a hand on the bottom holding a weapon on the top. The simplified character is just the left side of the original character, depicting a dagger made of wood.

shǎo 少 few; little (in quantity); seldom

*Few people **show** you their treasures.*

shǎo is said with the third tone/low rising tone. When you only have a few things in your pocket, you have to reach down deep to dig them out.

少 When you have something small (小) and then take a slice out of it, in this case represented by the bottom stroke, you have very *little* left.

shātān 沙灘/沙滩 (sand) beach

*When you want a **sun tan**, you go to the beach.*

shātān is said with two first tones/high level tones. Beaches are always flat and level.

沙 This character means "sand." It has the "water" radical on the left, with少 as the phonetic on the right. Once again a phonetic was chosen that contributes to the meaning, since sand occurs on a beach where the water becomes 少 ("little," "scarce").

灘/滩 This character by itself means "beach." It too has the "water" radical on the left, with the character 難/难 on the right side as the phonetic.

shéi 誰/谁 who?

*Who is that **sha**dy character?*

shéi is said with the questioning intonation of the second tone (rising tone), appropriate for a question word like "who?"

誰/谁 The character has the "speech" radical on the left, since the question "who" is usually asked verbally. The phonetic on the right is the "short-tailed bird," used both as a phonetic and a radical in various characters. In the word 誰 it seems it's an owl emitting its cry of "who, who."

shén 神 God

*We should never **shun** anyone who doesn't believe in <u>God</u>.*

shén is said with the second tone/rising tone. When we worship God we often rise up in our pews to pray or sing hymns.

神 The character has the "God" radical on the left. When this radical appears on the left of a character, it looks a bit like a man in a necktie, turning to the right and heading to church. In reality it's a deliberate distortion of an altar (示) on which something (一) is placed on top as an offering to God.

The phonetic on the right side of 神 has a vertical line extending out from a farmer's field (田) and means "to extend." God extends his bounty to us, including the bounty of the fields.

shénme 甚麼/什么 what?

*When Jewish people recite prayers like "**shema** yisrael ..." those who don't understand Hebrew say "<u>What</u>?"*

shénme is said with the second tone/rising tone, the questioning intonation you might expect from a question word like "what?"

甚 The traditional version of this character looks a bit like a wheelbarrow, with the two long vertical lines as the handles on either side, the three sides of a rectangle on the very bottom representing the inside of the wheelbarrow, and the two short slanted strokes inside the rectangle depicting the contents of the wheelbarrow. All of this begs the question from a neighbor: "<u>What</u> is in the wheelbarrow?!"

什 The simplified character has the "people" radical on the left, since it is only people that ask "what is this?" before eating something. Cats and dogs will just eat it! The character for the number 10, 十, serves as the phonetic.

麼 The traditional version of this character has the character for "hemp" or "marijuana" (麻) on the top and an outline of a nose on the bottom, with a short stroke above it. A college dorm supervisor, sniffing marijuana smoke wafting toward his nose in the dorm, might well ask "_What_ is that?!"

么   The simplified version simply has the nose on the bottom with the small wisp of smoke on top, since that's the only character in the language to have that extra stroke on top of the nose.

shēntǐ   身體/身体   body

*We shouldn't **shun** anyone who doesn't have a <u>body</u> like Mr. **T**, nor should we **shun** people who don't look good in a **T**-shirt.*

shēntǐ is said with the first tone/high level tone followed by the third tone/low rising tone, as if you're looking over someone's body from head to toe with your voice.

身   This character depicts the body of a person, with the head facing left and the two legs striding forward on the bottom.

體/体   This character also means "body" in this rather redundant modern compound word. It has the "bone" radical on the left, showing flesh on the bottom housing the bones, which are depicted on top of the character. The simplified character has the "people" radical on the left, with the character 本, meaning "root," on the right. The body is the "root" of a person. 本 is written with the "tree" radical, to which is added an extra stroke on the bottom to emphasize the roots of the tree.

shì   是   to be (is; was; am; were; etc.)

*Chinese **sure** <u>is</u> a fascinating language!*

shì is said with the fourth tone/falling tone, in the decisive intonation we use when affirming we're <u>sure</u> of something.

是   The character seems to show people (人) on the bottom existing (being) under (下) the sun (日).

shíhou 時候/时候 time

*Ask Santa Claus at the mall if he'll be coming to your house at Christmas <u>time</u>, and he'll definitely answer "<u>**Sure, ho**</u>, ho, ho!"*

shíhou is said with the second tone/rising tone, as if someone asks you what time it is, and you answer, "Time? Why it's 12:00."

時/时 This character by itself means "time." It has the "sun" radical on the left, since before cellphones and watches, people depended on the sun to know what time of day it was. The traditional character has the character 寺, which means "Buddhist temple," as the phonetic on the right. The striking of the bells in the temples at certain times of day announces the hours of prayer. 寺 does look a bit like a hand on the bottom with a wrist watch on the top. In the simplified version, the phonetic is reduced to just the hand on the right, perhaps pointing to the angle of the sun to indicate the time of day.

候/候 This character was added in the modern language to avoid confusion in speech between several hundred other characters that have a similar pronunciation. It is used as a suffix in a number of compound words in Chinese, including the word for "to wait." Since human beings spend a great deal of their time waiting, this seemed an appropriate suffix to add in modern Chinese. The original meaning of the character was to wait on one's lord. The radical on the left is the "people" radical, representing the person attending the lord. On the bottom right is the "arrow" radical (矢), possibly symbolizing the hunt. What is directly above the arrow seems to be a sheath for the arrows, with the single vertical line just to the left perhaps representing one of the arrows. The original meaning seems to have been to wait upon one's lord during a hunt. By extension the meaning became simply "to wait" and is now used just as a suffix.

shìjiè 世界 the world

---

*We Christians believe **sure, Jesus** died for the sins of the world.*

shìjiè is said with two fourth tones/falling tones, as if getting an astronaut's view looking down on the world.

世 This character is a shorthand version of 三十, meaning "thirty," and by itself means "a generation," since a new generation is born every thirty years or so. Although there are a lot more than thirty countries in the world today, think of this character as representing the great multitude of nations in the world.

界 This character has the radical for "field" on top. From an agricultural perspective, the world is just one big field for raising crops. The phonetic on the bottom, 介, means "to introduce." It shows two people meeting under a roof. If we could introduce everyone in the world to one another, perhaps then we'd have a chance for world peace!

shìqing 事情 thing(s) [abstract things only]; events

---

*We're all **searching (sherching)** for some**thing** meaningful to do with our lives, but it's never a **sure thing** we'll find that meaningful thing to do.*

shìqing is said with the decisive-sounding fourth tone/falling tone, as if stating decisively the thing you've decided to do.

事 This character means "occurrence" or "thing" and shows a hand represented by the horizontal lines grasping a brush and writing things down.

情 This character was added in the modern language to avoid confusion between the over two hundred other Chinese words also pronounced *shi*. By itself this character means "feelings." Since we always have feelings about the things that happen to us, this seemed an appropriate suffix to add. The character has the "heart" radical on the left, apropos of feelings. The right side consists of the common phonetic 青. It is a general color word that can mean everything from "green" to "indigo." On the top of the character is a plant coming out of the ground, symbolizing the color green. The bottom part, written exactly like the moon, was originally written with the character 丹. It shows a crucible in which the red metal cinnabar was placed in an attempt to create the elixir of immortal life in ancient times.

As a mnemonic device, think about the feelings stirred in the heart upon seeing plants and flowers in the moonlight.

shǒu　手　hand(s)

*We often use our <u>hands</u> to **show** people what we mean.*

shǒu is said with the third tone/low rising tone, as if lowering something down into the palm of your hand.

手　The character shows the wrist, represented by the vertical line, with three fingers protruding.

shòu　瘦　thin; skinny

*People in a Broadway **show** tend to be very <u>thin</u>.*

shòu is said with the fourth tone/falling tone, as if a thin person is showing off their slender body by gesturing downward from head to toe.

瘦　This character is written with the "sickness" radical on the top and left side. In ancient China, where a large percentage of people were often starving due to famine, being fat showed you were well off and being skinny was often a sign of malnutrition and disease.

The phonetic part of the character has a hand on the bottom (又) and above it what appear to be two hands around the waist of a skinny person (臼), the body of whom is represented simply by one single vertical line.

shū 書／书 book(s)

*By the end of the school year, many students may be sick of studying and feel like saying to their <u>books</u> "**Shoo!** Get out of here!"*

shū is said with the first tone/high level tone, since we usually lay books flat on a high table or desk to read them.

書／书 The character 書 means "book." It shows a hand on the top holding a writing brush represented by the vertical line, with the bristles pressed down flat on the paper, writing down something that you want to say. Those words are represented by the mouth on the bottom of the character, with the horizontal line in the box representing the mouth filled with speech.

shù 數／数 number(s)

When you buy <u>shoes</u>, you have to know the <u>number</u> for the size you wear.

shù is said with the fourth tone/falling tone. Numbers should be called out in a decisive way, and the fourth tone is the decisive-sounding tone in Chinese.

數 The traditional character has two hands on the right, employed in counting the number of some object. The phonetic on the left has the "woman" radical and what appears to be a two-story building above. The idea was actually to show the women in the imperial harem, housed in a multi-storied building in the palace. Perhaps the hands are counting the number of women in that building.

数 The simplified character version replaces the two-story building with the character 米, meaning "rice." Perhaps the hands are counting the numbers of bushels of rice as well as of women!

shuō 說/说 to speak; say

I heard people say that guy is a real "__schmoe__." What does Joe __Schmoe__ have to say about that?!

shuō is said with the first tone/high level tone. When you speak, it should always be "on the level."

說/说 The character has the "speech" radical on the left, appropriately enough. On the right side is the classical Chinese word for "older brother," 兄, with what resembles horns on top and represents authority. When the older brother speaks, his younger siblings have to listen. The simplified character 说 uses a bare-bones outline of the "speech" radical on the left, which is true for the simplified versions of all characters with that radical.

suān 酸 sour

For all its beauty, a __swan__ has a __sour__ personality.

suān is said with the first tone/high level tone. Picture putting a lemon straight into your mouth!

酸 The character has the "alcohol" radical on the left. If alcohol isn't fermented properly, it turns into vinegar, which is sour. The character for vinegar also has the "alcohol" radical on the left. The phonetic on the right has a nose on top, a mustache underneath, and two legs on the bottom. Imagine a man with a mustache eating a lemon as he stands there and wrinkling his nose because of the sour taste.

suì 歲/岁 years of age

Our backs get more and more __swayed__ with __age__.

suì is said with the fourth tone/falling tone, as the years of our age weigh increasingly heavily upon us.

歲 The traditional character has a mountain (山) on top, a roof with a side wall below (厂), under which there is a distortion of the "foot-in-motion" radical (足) and a halberd (戈). Chinese books on etymology claim that this character originally showed the planet Jupiter, which the Chinese associated with war, much as the Romans did with the planet Mars. Since Jupiter's revolutions around the sun were calculated in years, the character came to mean "years," and, by extension, "years of age."

Remember the character by thinking that as we get older and time marches on, represented by the "foot" radical under the roof, the years seem to pile up into a mountain. Figuratively speaking, we begin to feel more and more wounded in body (the halberd), but hopefully not in spirit.

岁 The simplified version simply shows the moon descending down below the mountain, which is an unintentional but quite poetic way of portraying old age and death.

sùshè 宿舍 dormitory (dorm)

Sue, she lives in the dorm. Susie? She lives in the dorm, too.

sùshè is said with two fourth tones/falling tones. We fall into our beds in the dorm after studying Chinese all day, so the falling tones seem appropriate.

宿 This character means "to stay overnight." It has the "people" radical (人) and the character for "one hundred" (百) under a roof. Dorms provide sleeping places for several hundred people.

舍 This character means "house" or "dwelling." It features a slanted roof on top, with the character 舌, meaning "tongue," as the phonetic. Conversations are always going on in dorms. This character therefore literally means "housing for the night," i.e., a dormitory.

_tā_ 他; 她; 它　he; she; it

Ta-ta (bye, bye), there <u>she</u> goes!

_tā_ is said with the first tone/high level tone, as if pointing straight at the person who's saying "ta-ta" (goodbye) to you.

他; 她; 它　Until recently, the words for "he," "she," and "it" were all rendered with the character 他, which in classical Chinese simply met "other." This character has the "people" radical on the left, with the character 也, meaning "also," on the right. The notion behind this was that it referred to a person other than the speaker, in other words the person the speaker is speaking of, namely "he" or "she."

In the past half century or so, the character 她 came into use to mean "she" or "her," replacing the "woman" radical on the left for the "people" radical, and leaving 他 to just mean "he" or "his." At the same time, the character 它 was created to mean "it" or "its." It looks like a snake poised to strike with its tongue hanging out, under a roof.

tài 太　too

Thai *food is <u>too</u> spicy! And a* **tie** *is considered <u>too</u> formal in many situations these days.*

tài is said with the emphatic-sounding fourth tone/falling tone.

太　If you have something that's big (大) and you add something to it, in this case the little stroke protruding from the left leg of the person, you then have <u>too</u> much.

tàitài 太太 woman; lady; wife; Mrs.

My <u>wife</u> makes me wear a **tie** to church. <u>Women</u> seem to like men in a **tie**. My <u>wife</u> gave me a tie made in Thailand, which makes it a **Thai tie**!

tài is said with the emphatic-sounding fourth tone/falling tone, as if a wife is commanding her husband to put on a tie.

太太 If you have something that's big (大) and you add something to it, in this case the little stroke protruding from the left leg of the person, you then have <u>too</u> much. Put two of that character together and you get the idea of someone who is "too too" exalted, or "much too much," a respectful term for lady or wife or Mrs.

tāmen 他們/他们; 她們/她们; 它們/它们 they; them

Things are more **fun** with "-<u>men</u>," so you have more fun doing things with ***tāmen*** than with ***tā***.

tāmen is said with the first tone/high level tone followed by an empty tone.

他們/他们; 她們/她们; 它們/它们 The character 們 is used as a suffix on all of the singular pronouns in Chinese to make them plural. In this case, it changes "he," "she," and "it" to "they" or "those." The radical on the left side is the "people" radical, with the character for "door" or "gate," 門, as the phonetic on the right. The simplified character gives a bare-bones outline of the traditional character for "door" or "gate."

tāng 湯/汤 soup(s)

Hot-and-sour soup is a **tang**y <u>soup</u>.

tāng is said with the first tone/high level tone. You need to keep your soup level, so it won't spill over.

湯/汤 The character has the "water" radical on the left, since soup is a liquid. The phonetic on the right is a very common one in characters ending in the -*ang* sound. It shows the sun on top shooting its rays down on the earth. The simplified version is a bare-bones outline of the original.

táng 糖 candy; sugar

*SweetTarts and Tangy Tarts are very **tang**y <u>candy</u>.*

táng is said with the second tone/rising tone, as if inviting someone to enjoy a treat, asking "Candy?"

糖 The character has the "rice" radical 米 on the left, indicating the natural sweetness of rice and other grains. The phonetic on the right side looks like a hand feeding the mouth under a roof. The phonetic is the character for the Tang dynasty.

téng 疼 to hurt; to be painful

*When you bite your **tongue**, it <u>hurts</u>!*

téng is said with the second tone/rising tone, as if your doctor is asking you "painful?"

疼 This character has the "sickness" radical on the left, which looks like germs on the far left assailing the temple of the body. The phonetic under the roof is the character for "winter." On top of 冬 are threads tied at the end of the loom, with the "ice" radical on the bottom. Winter is the icy end of the year. This seems an appropriate phonetic for the character for "pain," since it is winter that usually brings us more aches and pains than the other seasons.

tī 踢 to kick; to play (soccer or football)

*On a windy day, the kicker on a football team has to **tee** up the ball to kick it.*

tī is said with the first tone/high level tone. In soccer, you kick the ball along the level playing field.

踢 The character has the "foot" radical on the left, with the character 易 on the right as the phonetic. The character 易 means "change." It shows a chameleon, with the head and four legs. A chameleon changes its color to blend in with its surroundings. When you kick a ball, it does change the position of the ball. But never kick a chameleon!

tīng 聽/听 to listen

*When I was young, I would listen for the **ting**-a-ling of the ice cream truck entering our street.*

ting is said with the first tone/high level tone. You should always listen with a high level of attention to whatever someone says to you.

聽 The traditional character is a combinational character made up of six different parts. It has a student or scholar character (壬) on the bottom left, listening to his teacher with his ear (耳), in order to make his heart (心) one (一) with his master's moral teachings, so that ten (十) eyes (目), i.e., a great many people, can see him be a person of high moral character. This one character not only contains the idea of listening, but also includes the ultimate higher purpose of listening.

听 The simplified character loses all of that profundity, although it is far easier to write. It substitutes the "mouth" radical on the left, since we listen to what other people say or "mouth off" to us. The fairly unhelpful phonetic on the right is the "axe" radical. A silly mnemonic device is, therefore, called for. The best I can do is "Axe (ask) me no questions, and you won't have to listen to my opinions!"

tǐyù　體育/体育　physical education

*If you want a body like Mr. **T.**, or want to look good in a **T**-shirt, **you** have to engage in **tǐyù**!*

tǐyù is said with the third tone/low rising tone followed by the fourth tone/falling tone. Vocally you're first bending down and touching your toes, then doing a jumping jack.

體　The traditional version of this character means "body." It has the "bone" radical on the left, showing flesh on the bottom that houses (the "roof" radical) the bones, which are depicted on top of the character.

体　The simplified character has the "people" radical on the left, with the character 本, meaning "root," on the right. The metaphor here is perhaps that the body is the "root" of a person. 本 is written with the "tree" radical, to which is added an extra stroke on the bottom to emphasize the roots of the tree.

育　This character means "to nurture." Under what appears to be a roof is a nose, below which is the "flesh" radical (月). The "flesh" radical looks exactly like the character for "moon," but is actually a deliberate distortion of the character for "meat" or "flesh," 肉. Therefore, think of the character 育 as nurturing a child, represented by its nose and fleshy body, under the roof of a home or school.

tōu　偷　to steal (stealthily)

*When a thief <u>steals</u> something, he gets up on his **toes** to creep quietly into the place he's robbing.*

tōu is said with the first tone/high level tone. What's being stolen is often up on a high shelf.

偷　The character has the "people" radical on the left. On the right is a roof, under which it appears a thief steals in with a knife (bottom right) in the light of the moon (bottom left).

COMMON CHINESE WORDS / 129

tóu 頭/头 head

*Some young children are **towheaded** children, with extremely light blond hair.*

tóu is said with the second tone/rising tone, as if with questioning intonation your doctor asks you where you might be feeling pain after a minor car accident: "Head?"

頭/头 The traditional form of the character shows the head on the right side, with 目 representing the face, wrinkle lines and all; the top of the skull is shown on top and the two lines on the bottom represent a beard. The phonetic on the left means "beans." The true etymology of the phonetic has to do with the fact that it shows a ritual vessel, with the 口 representing the mouth of the bowl or goblet. The simplified character seems to show a person (大) standing there with the two small lines on the top left pointing to the person's head.

wàitou 外頭/外头 outside

*When the weather is cold and you see a family member outside, you may ask "**Why** are you **outside**?!"*

wàitou is said with the fourth tone/falling tone followed by an empty tone, as if rain or snow is falling down onto your roof outside.

外 This character, which by itself means "outside," shows the crescent moon on the left and cracks in a tortoise shell on the right. In ancient China, future events were predicted by burning a tortoise shell to see where the cracks formed. This had to be done **outside** of the nighttime hours when the moon was in the sky, for the divination to be reliable.

頭/头 The traditional form of the character shows the head on the right side, with 目 representing the face, wrinkle lines and all; the top of the skull is shown on top and the two lines on the bottom represent a beard. The phonetic on the left means "beans." The true etymology of the phonetic has to do with the fact that it shows a ritual vessel, with the 口 representing the mouth of the bowl or goblet. The simplified character seems to show a person (大) standing there with the two small lines on the top left pointing to the person's head.

wán 完 to finish; to complete

*A person **won** the game, so it's finished. But when we <u>finished</u> the long game, the losers were all **wan** and pale.*

wán is said with the second tone/rising tone, as if asking someone, "Finished?"

完 The character has the "roof" radical on top. The actual idea was that when you finish building the walls of a house, you then put a roof on it. The phonetic on the bottom is the Chinese dollar character, 元.

wǎn 晚 late

*As it gets <u>late</u> in the day, the sun **wanes**.*

wǎn is said with the third tone/low rising tone, as if imitating the sun sinking in the west as the day wanes.

晚 The character has the "sun" radical on the left, since when the sun sets, the day is getting late. The phonetic on the right shows a rabbit, with its long ears on top of its head, and depicts its two long, jumpy legs. When the sun sets, the rabbits come out to feed, as the ancient Chinese observed.

wàn 萬/万 ten thousand

***I won!** I won <u>ten thousand</u> dollars!*

wàn is said with the decisive-sounding fourth tone/falling tone.

萬/万 The traditional character shows a scorpion, with the characteristic two appendages on the top of the head, written exactly like the "grass" radical. The bottom of the character shows the body and stinger of the scorpion. Although this pictograph was borrowed for its sound rather than having any connection to the meaning, when you lose $10,000 it certainly stings, as if you were stung by a scorpion! The simplified character looks like a person running to the right shouting "I won!"

wàng 忘 to forget

Never forget that there are close to fifty million people in mainland China alone with the surname Wang (Wang)!

wàng is said with the fourth tone/falling tone, since when we forget something it's like it's been flushed down into the deeper recesses of the mind.

忘 The character has the "heart" radical on the bottom, which also represents the "mind" in Chinese characters. The ancients believed that the heart was the seat of thought. The phonetic on top, 亡, shows a coffin and is a classical character that means "to die." When a thought dies in the heart or mind, you have forgotten it.

wár 玩兒/玩儿 to play; to have fun

Make wár, not war!

wár is said with the second tone/rising tone, as if swinging skyward on a swing.

玩 This character seems to show a king on the left side as a radical. A king does have a lot more resources for having fun than a commoner. It actually has the "jade" radical on the left, with the horizontal lines representing strings of precious gems. The original idea this character captures was to "play" or "amuse oneself" by admiring ornaments made of jade. The character for the Chinese dollar, 元, is the phonetic on the right side. It is hard to have fun without some money to spend!

兒/儿　The traditional character shows a boy, with the head on top and two slits for the eyes, with two legs on the bottom. The simplified version only shows the legs.

wáwa　娃娃　doll(s)

"**Wah wah**" *is the sound of a baby's cry, hence the actual derivation of this onomatopoeic word.*

wáwa is said with the second tone/rising tone, as if the baby's cry is rising up and reaching the ears of its parents.

娃　The character has the "woman" radical on the left, since most dolls are female. The phonetic on the right is shared by the word for frog, 蛙. Imagine it as shelves on which girls with lots of dolls might display them.

wàzi　襪子/袜子　socks

*Most of us tend to wad up our socks, and so have **wads** of socks in our drawers.*

wàzi is said with the fourth tone/falling tone, as if you're dropping your wadded up socks into your drawer.

襪/袜　Both the traditional and simplified versions of this character have the "clothing" radical on the left, appropriately enough. This radical is a deliberate distortion of 衣, the character for "clothing," to save room on the right for the phonetic. The complex phonetic in the traditional character has the "grass" radical on top, with an eye below, and two halberds on the bottom. Try to see the eye as a face with a straw hat, and the two halberds as legs, with the hash marks at the bottom of each as feet in need of socks. The simplified character substitutes the character 末 as a much simpler phonetic.

子　This character is a suffix that was added in the modern language and is a common ending on nouns.

wèile   爲了/为了   in order to; for the purpose of

*In order to **wail**, I went to the Wailing Wall.*

wèile is said with the fourth tone/falling tone, as if stating confidently your purpose for doing something.

爲/为   This character means "for the sake of" and shows a mother monkey with one forepaw raised above its head. Below her forepaw is her head and breast. Her feet are on the very bottom. The explanation is that the mother monkey does a great deal for the sake of her child, just as a human mother does. The simplified version is simply a very bare outline of the original character.

wēixiǎn   危險/危险   dangerous

*I'm **seeing** it as **way** too **dangerous**!*

wēixiǎn is said with the first tone/high level tone followed by the third tone/low rising tone, as if a person is on a high cliff and then falls down to the bottom.

危   This character by itself means "precipitous" or "dangerous." It actually shows a person on top of a cliff (⌐) looking down at a person curled up at the bottom, symbolizing danger.

險/险   This character by itself also means "precarious" or "dangerous." The radical on the left shows earth piled up. You can look at this character as if it is Humpty Dumpty, with its head and belly facing right. We all know how dangerous that wall of bricks proved for Humpty Dumpty! In the traditional character, the phonetic appears to be a threatening pumpkin face, with two eyes and two jagged teeth under the lid of the pumpkin. The simplified version reduces the eyes and teeth to just four strokes.

wèn 問/问 to ask

*We often <u>ask</u> the question "<u>**When**</u>?"*

wèn is said with the fourth tone/falling tone, as if you pour a drink for a friend and ask them to say "when," and they respond "when" with a decisive tone.

> 问/问 The character has the "mouth" radical (口) in the middle of the "door" radical (門) in this combinational character with two radicals and no phonetic. When someone knocks on our door, we <u>ask</u> "who's there?" The simplified version gives a bare-bones outline of the "door" radical (门).

wǒ 我 I; me

*Oh, <u>**woe**</u> is <u>me</u>!*

wǒ is said with the third tone/low rising tone, as if dropping your voice low out of modesty when speaking about yourself.

> 我 The character shows a hand on the left (手) holding a weapon called the halberd (戈) on the right, which could be used to defend one's own land and property. By extension it came to mean oneself, i.e., "I."

wǒmen 我們/我们 we; us

*Whether <u>we</u> are <u>**wǒmen**</u> or men, <u>we</u> are all one race, the human race. And things are much more fun with "men" (們/们)!*

wǒ is said with the third tone/low rising tone, followed by an empty tone, as if dropping your voice low out of modesty when speaking about yourself.

> 我 The character shows a hand on the left (手) holding a weapon called the halberd (戈) on the right, which could be used to defend one's own land and property. By extension it came to mean oneself, i.e., "I."

> 們 This character is used as a suffix on all the singular pronouns in Chinese to make them plural. The radical on the left

side is the "people" radical, with the character for "door" or "gate," 門, as the phonetic on the right. The simplified character gives a bare-bones outline of the traditional character for "door" or "gate."

wòshì　臥室/卧室　bedroom

*Even if you don't have a **washer** or dryer in your bedroom, **wòshì** still means "bedroom" in Chinese.*

wòshì is said with the fourth tone/falling tone. The bedroom is where you fall into bed, after all!

臥/卧　The traditional version of this character by itself means "to lie prostrate." It shows the outline of an official kowtowing on the left, with the character for "person" on the right. An official is a person who must prostrate himself before the emperor. By extension the character came to mean "lie down." The simplified character substitutes for the person on the right the cracks in a tortoise shell that were used for divination.

室　This character means "room" and is just used as a suffix with words for various types of rooms. It has the "roof" radical on top. The phonetic on the bottom, 至, means "to arrive." It shows a bird nose-diving down to a place on the ground (土). A room is a place under a roof at which one arrives.

wǔfàn　午飯/午饭　lunch

*I **wolf** down my lunch, because I'm a big **fan** of food!*

wǔfàn is said with the third tone/low rising tone followed by the fourth tone/falling tone. First you pick up your lunch from down on the table, then drop it into your mouth.

午　This character probably shows a sundial, with the sun directly overhead at noon and casting the fairly vertical shadow shown by the top left stroke. However, you might think of it as ten o'clock (十), eleven o'clock (add 一 on top), twelve o'clock rock!

飯/饭　This character has the "food" radical on the left. 反, which means "to turn over," is the phonetic on the right. It shows a hand (又), with palm down, being turned over, the motion of which is represented by the two-stroke character 厂. The phonetic slightly resembles a little tray table on which you might place a meal. The simplified character is exactly the same, except that the "food" radical on the left has been pared down.

xī　西　west

See *the sun set in the* <u>*west*</u>*.*

xī is said with the first tone/high level tone, as if symbolizing the sun setting in the west just above the horizon, on the level with your line of vision.

西　This character actually shows the belly and long legs of a sea bird inside its nest. When the sun sets in the west, the birds go to their nests to rest.

xǐ　洗　to wash

See *how clean it is after I* <u>*washed*</u> *it.*

xǐ is said with the third tone/low rising tone, as if lowering dishes or clothing into soapy water to wash them.

洗　This character has the "water" radical on the left. The phonetic on the right, 先, looks like a person holding a towel or washcloth on the top left who is walking into the bathroom to wash. 先 means "first" and depicts a person walking ahead of another. It is true, of course, that when you wash, the first thing you need to do is find some water.

xiān 先 first

CNN used to deliver the news <u>first</u>, before every other news network.

xiān is said with the first tone/high level tone, as befitting a word that means "first."

先 The character shows a person walking (儿) on the ground (土). The line on the top left indicates that the person has reached that spot first, before the people presumed to be on his right who are trying to reach that same spot.

xiànzài 現在/现在 now; the present

*I'm <u>**seein'**</u> you <u>now</u> with my own <u>**eyes**</u>.*

xiànzài is said with two fourth tones/falling tones, with the decisive intonation you would expect for an emphatic word like "right now."

現/现 This character by itself means "the present moment." It has the "jade" radical on the left, and the character 見, meaning "to see," on the right. The 見 radical is composed of an eye (目) on two legs, which also contributes to the meaning of the character. Originally, this character was meant to capture the act of looking and admiring a piece of jade. The simplified version pushes the two legs up into the eye.

在 This character means "to be at" or "in ..." This word refers to a location and shows a place on the ground (土) under a shelter.

xiǎo 小 little; small

See 'ow little *I am, Henry Higgins (Eliza Doolittle might have said in "My Fair Lady").*

xiǎo is said with the third tone/low rising tone, as if bending down to reach a small object on the ground.

小 The character actually shows a person with arms down by her/his side, looking small.

xiào 笑 to laugh

See 'ow *I'll* laugh, *Henry Higgins, when the king orders "Off with Henry Higgin's head!" (paraphrase of line from Eliza Doolittle's song in "My Fair Lady," "Just You Wait, Henry Higgins, Just You Wait!").*

xiào is said with the fourth tone/falling tone. Since laughter is generally done emphatically, it is logical that it's said with the decisive falling tone.

笑 The character has the "bamboo" radical on top, with the phonetic 夭, meaning "to die prematurely," on the bottom. The actual reason for using the "bamboo" radical in the character "to laugh" is that when people really belly laugh, they shake like bamboo does in the wind. The phonetic on the bottom looks a bit like a person laughing his head off.

xiě 寫/写 to write

In an e-mail or letter we often write *"*see ya *soon!"*

xiě is said with the third tone/low rising tone, perhaps to mimic the lowering of a writing brush down on paper.

寫/写 The traditional character shows a magpie under a roof. The original concept of this word was that the magpie is a bird that makes its nest in a very orderly, neat fashion. Likewise, those who write should carefully order their thoughts before putting them down on paper.

The character looks a bit like a student writing a term paper on a computer under a roof, with the head directly below the roof and the fingers on the keyboard at the very bottom of the character. The simplified character is a bare-bones outline of the original character, and removes the roof tile on top of the traditional character.

xièxiè   謝謝/谢谢   thank-you

See ya how *thankful* I am to you?

xièxiè is said with two fourth tones/falling tones, with the decisive intonation of the falling tone.

謝/谢   This character has the "speech" radical on the left, since thanks are so often given verbally. The phonetic on the right, 射, seems to contribute to the meaning. It's composed of the character for "body," 身, on the left, and the character for "inch," 寸, on the right. The Chinese traditionally bow, inching the body forward, when saying thank you. This word is generally repeated twice to make it is clear which *xiè* is being said. Therefore the character is written twice in this expression, to reflect the spoken language.

xǐhuān   喜歡/喜欢   to like

If you **see Juan**, my Puerto Rican friend, you will *like* him. And if you **see San Juan**, Puerto Rico, you will *like* that, too!

xǐhuān is said with the third tone/low rising tone followed by the first tone/high level tone. It's as if you shyly tell someone you like them, lowering your voice to the bottom of your range before coming back up.

喜   This character means "happy" or "happiness." It seems to show 11 (10 + 1) mouths on top and 20 mouths on the bottom, representing a great many people eating, drinking, and singing happily at a party. That is actually not too different from the true etymology of the character. The character on the bottom does show a great many mouths drinking and singing at a celebration. The top part, however, actually shows the head of a drum being beaten in time to the singing at the party.

歡/欢   This character also means "happy" or "to rejoice." The radical on the right shows a person on the bottom with breath rising up, exhaling as if to say "oh joy, oh rapture!" The phonetic on the left depicts an osprey or other sea bird with the "short-tailed bird" radical on the bottom. The radical has two eyes above it and the plumage on the head rises to the very top of the character. In its simplified version this phonetic is always reduced to just two strokes and looks like the character 又, which shows the palm of a hand facing down. Appropriate enough, since when we like something, we often clap our hands to show our approval.

xīn   新   new

Sin is nothing new in the world, but xīn is!

xīn is said with the first tone/high level tone. Newness implies a beginning, and the four tones of Chinese begin with the first tone.

新   This character has the "axe" radical on the right, showing the handle on the bottom right and the blade of the axe on the top and left side. The actual idea was that in order to make a new home for yourself, you have to hew wooden beams with an axe. The phonetic on the right, used notably in the character 親/亲, meaning "relative," seems to contribute to the meaning. The simplified and traditional forms of 親/亲 are both written with the character meaning "to stand," 立, on the top, and the character for "tree," 木, on the bottom. When you use an axe to make a new home for yourself, you must first cut down the trees standing there to clear a space.

xìn 信 letter(s); to believe in ...

---

*It's a **sin** to not write **letters** to those you love!*

xìn is said with the fourth tone/falling tone. When you believe in something, you state your faith in it most emphatically. The falling tone in Chinese is the emphatic one. And when you put a letter in the mailbox, you drop it in and let it fall.

> 信 The character is written with the "people" radical on the left and the "speech" radical on the right. The original idea was that a person's words should be sincere and therefore believable. By extension the character came to mean "to believe in (something)." In modern Chinese, as a noun it came to have the more prosaic meaning of "a letter," which in fact is composed of words written by a person.

xíng 行 O.K.; fine

---

*When everything is going **fine**, we often will start to **sing**!*

xíng is said with the second tone/rising tone, as if asking if something is O.K. using the querulous second tone.

> 行 The word *xíng* originally meant "to go," a meaning it retains in some compound words. It actually depicts two footprints, but looks like an intersection of two streets. By extension it came to mean, figuratively speaking, that an idea or suggestion "goes" along with the opinion of others. Hence the modern meaning of "O.K."

xìng 姓 surname (last name); to be surnamed

---

*A drill sergeant in the army might command his men: "**Sing** out your **names**, boys!"*

xìng is said with the fourth tone/falling tone, since we state our last name with the decisive- and confident-sounding fourth tone.

> 姓 The character has the "woman" radical on the left with the character 生, meaning "to be born," on the right. When

we are given birth by a woman, we automatically receive a last name, even if we aren't immediately given a first name.

xīngqī 星期 week

String cheese is good any day of the *week*! And in the U.S. we're *seeing cheese* every day of the *week* in the dishes we eat.

xīngqī is said with two first tones/high level tones. The first tone in Chinese is the longest, most drawn-out one, as if hinting at how long a week can seem.

星 This character means "star." It shows our star, the sun, on top, with 生 as the phonetic on the bottom.

期 This character means "period of time." It has the "moon" radical on the left, which by itself means "month," with the phonetic 其 on the right. 星期 literally means "star date." It is the 20th-century word for "week" and replaced the older term, 礼拜 , which also means "worship" and was invented by the Jesuit astronomers in the 16th century. The term 星期 was created to sound more modern and to lose the religious connotations of 礼拜 in a society that taught that religion was the opiate of the masses.

xǐshǒu 洗手 wash one's hands

I'll *show* you my *hands* and you can *see* how clean I've *washed* them.

xǐshǒu is said with two third tones/low rising tones, as if symbolizing dipping one's hands into soapy water to wash them again and again.

洗 This character has the "water" radical on the left. The phonetic on the right, 先, looks like a person holding a towel or washcloth on the top left who is walking into the bathroom to wash. 先 means "first" and depicts a person walking ahead of another. It is true, of course, that when you wash, the first thing you need to do is find some water.

手 This character shows the wrist, represented by the vertical line, with three fingers protruding.

xiūxi 休息 to rest

See, oh, see how I need to rest.

xiūxi is said with the first tone/high level tone. We prefer to rest stretched out flat on a high level surface like a bed or sofa.

休 This character by itself means "to rest." It actually depicts a person resting under a tree.

息 This character means "breath." It shows the nose on top, inhaling and giving breath to the heart on the bottom of the character.

xǐzǎo 洗澡 to bathe/shower

*Mom **sees how** clean I am after bathing, a child might say.*

xǐzǎo is said with two third tones (low rising tones), as if mimicking lowering oneself down into the bathtub to bathe—not once, but twice, since the first time the water seemed too hot.

洗 This character has the "water" radical on the left. The phonetic on the right, 先, looks like a person holding a towel or washcloth on the top left who is walking into the bathroom to wash. 先 means "first" and depicts a person walking ahead of another. It is true, of course, that when you wash, the first thing you need to do is find some water.

澡 This character also has the "water" radical on the left. The phonetic on the right looks a bit like three cakes of soap on top, with the "tree" radical on the bottom representing a tub made of wood.

xué 學/学 to study; to learn

*How **sweet** it is to <u>study</u> and to <u>learn</u>.*

xué is said with the second tone/rising tone. Your voice rises up, mirroring your aspirations to elevate your ability in the subject you're learning.

學/学 The traditional version of this character shows two hands on either side of the top part, passing down knowledge to the student below, who is like a child (子) in his or her ignorance. The roof over the child's head seems to represent the confines of the student's mind. Studying will hopefully remove the roof, the barrier to learning, and allow true knowledge to enter. The simplified version reduces the entire top half of the character to three simple strokes.

xūyào 需要 to need

*Americans are a litigious people, who it seems <u>need</u> to **sue you** at the drop of a hat.*

xūyào is said with the first tone/high level tone followed by the fourth tone/falling tone. It's as if you feel a need to obtain something high in value to you (first tone) and then express your desire for it with the decisive fourth tone.

需 This character has the "rain" radical on top, with what appears to be a rake on the bottom. Crops <u>need</u> both rain and cultivation to thrive.

要 This character by itself means "to need" as well as "to want" or "will ..." Every woman (女) wants or needs her own nest (西). This character actually shows a woman putting her hands around her waist, and originally meant a person's waist-line. It was later borrowed for its sound, the word "to want" being a homonym with the word for "waist." The word for "waist" is now written with the "flesh" radical on the left (腰).

yáng 羊 sheep

A ***yang*** *and yinnocent (young and innocent)* <u>sheep</u>.

yáng is said with the second tone/rising tone, as if calling for sheep that have gone astray.

羊 The character shows the horns of a ram on top, with the body of the sheep represented by the rest of the character.

yào 要 to want

<u>Yow</u>*! When you* <u>want</u> *something really badly, it hurts.*

yào is said with the fourth tone/falling tone, with the same intonation as when we exclaim "Yow!" in English when we're in pain.

要 This character by itself means "to need" as well as "to want" or "will ..." Every woman (女) wants or needs her own nest (西). This character actually shows a woman putting her hands around her waist, and originally meant a person's waistline. It was later borrowed for its sound, the word "to want" being a homonym with the word for "waist." The word for "waist" is now written with the "flesh" radical on the left (腰).

yāzi 鴨子/鸭子 duck

<u>yā</u> *imitates the hoarse sound of a* <u>duck</u>*'s quack.*

yāzi is said with the first tone/high level tone, with the voice flat and level, like a duck floating on the water.

鴨/鸭 This character has the "bird" radical on the right, showing the head of a bird on top with a crest. The body of the bird is below and ends with a long tail, which is represented by the bottom four strokes. The phonetic on the left shows a tortoise shell.

子 This character is a common suffix for a great many nouns in Chinese.

yě 也 also; too

*Oh, **yeah**, there's **yet** another thing also.*

yě is said with the third tone/low rising tone, dipping low with the voice in this word that indicates an afterthought.

也 Etymologists believe this character was actually the rough outline of a jar or pot, and was borrowed for its sound.

yèlǐ 夜裏/夜里 night; in the night

*You can **yell "ee!"** in the **night**, but they won't hear you!*

yèlǐ is said with the fourth tone/falling tone followed by the third tone/low rising tone. It sounds like night falling and then settling in.

夜 This character by itself means "night." It shows a person under a roof at night, with the moon stealing in on the bottom right, as if on legs.

裏/里 The traditional version of this character has the "clothing" radical (衣) split with the phonetic 里. The original idea really was something "inside" a garment. The phonetic 里, meaning "mile," combines the "field" radical on the top with the character for "earth" or "ground" on the bottom. The idea was actually to measure the land in the fields in *miles*. The simplified character for "inside" just uses the phonetic.

yěxǔ 也許/也许 maybe; perhaps

Yes, you—maybe!

yěxǔ is said with two third tones/low rising tones, in the resigned intonation of a word meaning "perhaps."

也 Etymologists believe this character was actually the rough outline of a jar or pot, and was borrowed for its sound.

許/许 The character 許 means "to permit." It has the "speech" radical on the left. The phonetic on the right, 午,

means "noon." It shows a sundial with the shadow of the sun directly overhead, indicated by the stroke on the top left. 也許 literally means "also permitted," i.e., "also possible," and by extension came to mean "maybe" and "perhaps."

yéye 爺爺/爷爷 paternal grandfather

*Grandparents tend to be much more permissive than parents. Grandpa will often say to his grandchildren "**Yeah, yeah**, of course you may!"*

yéye is said with the second tone/rising tone, as if asking your grandpa if you can have something.

爺/爷 The traditional form of this character contains the character for "father" (父) as the radical. 父 shows father standing there with his arms raised above his head in a show of authority. The phonetic on the bottom of 爺 has the "ear" radical on the bottom left side and the "city wall" radical on the bottom right. Think of how grandpa sits there with his slightly big belly, in this case the "city wall" radical, listening to you with his one good ear.

yīfu 衣服 clothes; clothing

*In China as in the U.S., **if you** don't wear clothing in public, you get arrested!*

yīfu is said with the first tone/high level tone. You should always lay your clothing out flat, so it won't get wrinkled.

衣 This character by itself means "clothing." It shows the neckline and inner seams of a garment.

服 This character was added in the modern language to avoid confusion with so many other words that are homonyms. 服 has the "flesh" radical on the left, with what appears to be a hook for hanging clothes on the top right and a small stool on the bottom right. A person enters a fitting room in a department store to try on clothing to put on their body (月),

while sitting on the stool and putting their own clothes on the hook above.

yǐjīng 已經/已经 already

*We're <u>already</u> **eating**.*

yǐjīng is said with the third tone/low rising tone followed by the first tone/high level tone. Dipping low with your voice, then coming back up to a high level pitch, seems to reflect having gone to do something and returned from having done it.

已 This character by itself means "already." It shows a silkworm curled up, all ready to make its cocoon from which silk is made.

經/经 This character was added to avoid confusion with other homophonic words. This character means "to pass through." It has the "silk" radical on the left. Silk has to pass through a number of processes before it is made into a garment. The phonetic on the right shows water passing through an underground passage. The simplified form of the phonetic looks like a person on the top walking to work (工) in a silk factory, where many silk garments have <u>already</u> been produced.

yīngdāng 應當/应当 ought to; should

*You <u>ought to</u> get off your **ying-yang** and get to work!*

yīngdāng is said with two first tones/high level tones. When you tell a person that they ought to do something, you're saying that they should aim for a high level of accomplishment.

應/应 This character by itself means "should." It has the "heart" radical on the bottom, since we know in our hearts what we should do. The phonetic on the top has the "roof with sidewall" radical on the top and left side, with the "people" radical and the "short-tailed bird" radical inside. This phonetic represents the eagle, a bird that builds a "home" (nest) almost as large as that of a human. The simplified character is a very sketchy outline of the original character.

當/当 This character was added as a suffix in the modern language to avoid confusion with other homophonic words. It has the "field" radical on the bottom, with the rather common phonetic 尚 on top. That phonetic shows the slanted roof tiles, the roof, and a window, and is found in a number of characters that end with the -ang sound. The simplified version looks a bit like the head of a turkey!

yīnggāi 應該/应该 ought to; should

*Hey, **guy**! You <u>ought to</u> get off your **ying**-yang and get to work!*

yīnggāi is said with two first tones/high level tones. When you tell a person that they ought to do something, you're saying that they should aim for a high level of accomplishment.

應/应 This character by itself means "should." It has the "heart" radical on the bottom, since we know in our hearts what we should do. The phonetic on the top has the "roof with sidewall" radical on the top and left side, with the "people" radical and the "short-tailed bird" radical inside. This phonetic represents the eagle, a bird that builds a "home" (nest) almost as large as that of a human. The simplified character is a very sketchy outline of the original character.

該/该 This character was added in modern Chinese to avoid confusion with other homophonic words. It has the "speech" radical on the left, since we usually tell someone verbally what they should do. The phonetic on the right shows a pig with head, four legs, and a tail that is turned 90 degrees to better fit with the "speech" radical. This is a common phonetic in characters read *hai*, *gai*, etc., including the character for child 孩.

yínháng 銀行 bank

In hanging onto your money, you should deposit it in a <u>bank</u>.

yínháng is said with two second tones/rising tones, as if asking directions to a bank with querulous rising tones.

银   This character means "silver" and contains the "gold" radical on the left, which is the radical for all metals as well as objects made of metal. It looks a bit like a bank teller, with the head facing to the right and legs on the bottom. You can also think of this character as a rice bowl on top, squared off, with a silver spoon or ladle on the bottom.

行   This character has two readings. Besides the more common meaning of "to go," it is also read as *háng* in compounds referring to a profession. While resembling an intersection of two roads, this character actually shows two footprints, metaphorically representing the career path one takes in life.

yìqǐ 一起 together

When we were <u>together</u> in the garden, we all brushed against poison ivy. Now we're all **<u>itchy</u>** <u>together!</u>

yìqǐ is said with the fourth tone/falling tone followed by the third tone/low rising tone. It's as if a group of people jump down into a swimming pool together.

一   This character means "one," but you probably already knew that.

起   The character means "to rise up." It has the character 走, meaning "to go," on the left, which shows a character that looks like a foot on the bottom (止), with the heel and sole of the foot raised, walking along the ground (土). The phonetic on the right looks like a silk worm crawling upward.

yīsheng 醫生/医生 physician; doctor

---

*"EE, that **stung**!" is what many of us say when the <u>doctor</u> gives us a shot.*

yīsheng is said with the first tone/high level tone, with a long, drawn-out "ee" cried out in pain.

醫/医 This character broadly means "medicine" or "medical." It actually shows on the top left a wound made in the human body by an arrow (矢), which is removed by a hand (又) on the top right holding a scalpel or other instrument. That hand then disinfects the wound with alcohol (酒), which is pictured on the bottom minus the "water" radical. Since this is the only character in the Chinese language with that top left part, the simplified character is reduced to just that.

生 This character is a suffix commonly added to nouns regarding people, such as 学生 for student. Among its many meanings is the idea of "scholar." Therefore an 醫生/医生 literally means "medical scholar."

yòng 用 to use

---

*Psychologists still <u>use</u> the teachings of Carl **Jung** along with those of Sigmund Freud.*

yòng is said with the fourth tone/falling tone. When we use some tool like a hammer, we let it fall forcefully from above.

用 This character actually shows a hand, palm down, holding some sort of tool. Think of it as a chess or checkerboard that we use for those games, because that's what it resembles.

yǒude   有的   some ...

---

*In "Star Wars" <u>some</u> characters are named <u>**Yoda**</u> and <u>some</u> are not.*

yǒude is said with the third tone/low rising tone, as if reaching deep down in your pocket or purse for some coins.

有   This character means both "to have" and "there is/there are." It seems to show a hand holding the moon. But the hand is actually holding a piece of meat, which was a rare thing in ancient China for most people to have, outside of a New Year's feast, given how expensive it was.

的   This character is used to create the idea "there are some ...," i.e., "some ..."

yuán   圓/元   the Chinese dollar

<u>**You when**</u> *are going to give me the <u>dollar</u> you owe me?!*

yuán is said with the second tone/rising tone, as if asking for money.

圓   The traditional version of this character originally meant "round," a meaning that it still retains in modern usage. It was written with a circle, referring to metal coins. It is now written with the "enclosure" radical, whose rectangular shape resembles a Chinese dollar bill. The phonetic inside looks a bit like the head, body, and legs of a bank teller, giving you some paper bills.

元   The simplified character uses another character that means "first" or "elemental." Since the Chinese dollar is an elemental part of Chinese currency, and because it is so much easier to write, this homophonic character now means the Chinese dollar. Think of it as showing a person walking away from the bank with a single dollar (一).

yuǎn 遠/远 far; distant

*The **U.N.** is far from China.*

yuǎn is said with the third tone/low rising tone, as your voice travels rather far, dipping low and then rising up again.

遠 The traditional version of this character has the "foot" radical on the left, with a fairly common phonetic on the right found in characters read *yuan*. The phonetic appears to have the "earth" radical on the left, below which is a person with head, legs, and arms traveling to a distant place. However, when the "earth" radical is found on the top of a character, it generally is a distortion of the head of a person. The phonetic actually shows the head and flowing garments of an official being sent to a distant province to take up his new office. Thus once again a phonetic was chosen which contributes to the meaning of the entire character.

远 In the simplified version, the phonetic is replaced by the homophonic character 元, which appears to be a person walking to a faraway place on two legs, with the head simply suggested by the one line on top.

yuē 約/约 appointment; date

*Will **you, uh**, have a date with me?*

yuē is said with the first tone/high level tone. You and the person with whom you make a date should be on the same high level as fellow human beings.

約/约 This character has the "silk" radical on the left, with a hook on the right. When you make an appointment, date, or agreement with someone, you are figuratively bound to one another, as if tied together with silk thread. And you're on the hook to follow through with the appointment or date you have set up.

yǔfǎ   語法/语法   grammar

You can't get *far* in learning a language without knowing the *grammar*.

yǔfǎ is said with two third tones/low rising tones. You need to really get to the bottom of the grammar of a language to really learn to speak that language properly.

語/语   The character 語/语 means "language." It has the "speech" radical on the left. The phonetic on the right was the word for "I" or "me" in classical Chinese. The character 吾 is comprised of the "mouth" radical, with the character for the number 5, 五, as its phonetic.

法   The character 法 means "way" as well as "law." It has the "water" radical on the left, with the character 去, meaning "to go," on the right. Water flows in certain ways or channels. So too should the behavior of humans be channeled by laws.

yùxí   預習/预习   prepare lessons before class (for students)

At *U.C.*-Berkeley, a top-notch school, students *always prepare their lessons before class*. The teachers then tell them: "*You see* how important it is to *prepare for class!*"

yùxí is said with the fourth tone/falling tone, followed by the second tone/rising tone. You prepare for Chinese class in part by writing the characters in the new lesson, letting the pen drop down on a piece of paper, then lifting it up.

預/预   This character has the "head" radical on the right side, representing the idea of doing something a*head* of time. The phonetic on the left, 予, means "to give." It resembles the character for "child," 子, with which it shouldn't be confused. However, as a mnemonic device, think about children preparing their lessons ahead of time.

習/习   This character means "to study" or "to learn." It has the two wings of a bird on top, with the character for "white," 白, on the bottom. The metaphor seems to be a baby bird that has a white belt (is a novice) in flying, testing its wings as it learns to fly.

zhàn 站 to stand

We often have to <u>stand</u> outside a "__john__" for a chance to use a public restroom.

zhàn is said with the fourth tone/falling tone. When we stand upright, we hold our bodies vertically. The falling tone has a fittingly vertical feel to it.

站 On the left side of this character is an outline of a person standing upright, with two slanted vertical lines representing their legs. The phonetic on the right side looks like a sign at a taxi stand. It actually shows the mouth of a soothsayer on the bottom, with the top two strokes representing cracks on a tortoise shell or deer bone, which were used for divination in ancient China.

zhàngfu 丈夫 husband

A lot of <u>husbands</u> eat a lot of __junk food__!

zhàngfu is said with the decisive-sounding fourth tone/falling tone, as befits the man who thinks, at least, that he's the head of the household.

丈 This character means "man." It shows a man striding forward confidently.

夫 This character also means "man" and like the character丈 implies manliness. 夫 portrays a man who, to all appearance, has two sets of arms, emphasizing strength and robustness.

zhèlǐ 這裏/这里 here

That person is <u>here</u> in <u>jail</u>.

zhèlǐ literally means "in this (place)." *zhèlǐ*, meaning "this," is said with the decisive-sounding fourth tone/falling tone, as if confidently pointing to something and saying "this." *lǐ*, meaning "in(side)," is said with the third tone/low rising tone, reflecting putting something down into your pocket or purse.

> 這/这   Think of a policeman warning you not to *jay*walk. The right side of the simplified version looks a bit like a person *jay*walking.

> 裏/里   The traditional version of this character has the "clothing" radical (衣) split with the phonetic 里. The original idea really was something "inside" a garment. The phonetic 里, meaning "mile," combines the "field" radical on the top with the character for "earth" or "ground" on the bottom. The idea was actually to measure the land in the fields in <u>miles</u>. The simplified character for "inside" just uses the phonetic.

zhèngfǔ 政府 government

While many husbands eat junk food, the <u>government</u> cautions us to not eat a lot of <u>junk food</u>.

zhèngfǔ is said with the fourth tone/falling tone, followed by the third tone/low rising tone. Most elected governments start at the top in popular opinion, only to have their ratings fall to the bottom near the end of their administration.

> 政   This character means "to govern" or "to administer" and is therefore used in words related to political affairs. It shows two hands on the right as the radical, representing the power of those who govern. The phonetic on the left is a fairly common one in characters read *zheng*. 正 by itself means "just" in every sense of the word in English. It shows a foot (止) stopping <u>just</u> at a certain line (一). All governments, to one extent

or another, make their citizens "toe the line." But hopefully they are "just."

府 This character means "official residence" or "mansion." It is written with the radical 广, which shows a roof with a single roof tile and a side wall. The phonetic inside, 付, means "to pay." It shows a person on the left paying money with the hand pictured on the right. Since citizens all have to pay taxes to their government, the choice of phonetic seems significant. And because those who are in power in any government live in a special official residence, the compound word for "government" in Chinese literally means "political mansion" or "official residence of those who govern."

zhīdào 知道 to know

We <u>know</u> the **jerks** who make the big money from the **<u>Dow</u>** (Jones) are not the typical investors.

zhīdào is said with the first tone/high level tone followed by the fourth tone/falling tone. When you know something, your knowledge is on a fairly high level (first tone). You can then state what you know with confidence (fourth tone).

知 This character by itself means "to know." It has the "mouth" radical on the right, since we often verbally state what we know. The phonetic on the left, 矢, depicts an arrow. When you know something, you can speak about it swiftly and precisely, like an arrow hitting its mark.

道 This character means "path" or "way." It has the "foot" radical on the left, with the character for "head" in classical Chinese on the right. This combinational character means "the head or main path to take," i.e., "the way." 道 was added as a suffix to this entry to avoid confusion in the spoken language with the many other homophonic characters.

zhōng 鍾/钟 clock

This word originally meant the large bell struck in bell towers in ancient China to announce the time of day. It imitates the sound of a bell being struck. In modern Chinese the word has come to mean "clock."

zhōng is said with the first tone/high level tone, perhaps because when you strike a bell, you do it with a high, level motion.

鍾/钟 This character is written with the "gold" radical on the left, since bells and clocks were originally made of metal. The phonetic in the traditional character, 重, means "heavy." It seems an appropriate phonetic, since bells as well as ancient clocks were heavy objects. The character 重 seems to show weights piled up, as they would be at a gym. In the simplified version of the character 钟, the phonetic 重 is replaced with the simpler character 中 .

zhòng 重 heavy

zhòng seems to be the sound of a heavy object dropped down on the ground, where it lands with a thud.

zhòng is said with the fourth tone/falling tone, as if you are dropping a heavy object down onto the ground.

重 This character seems to show weights piled up, as they would be at a gym.

zhū 猪 pig

*It's ironic that the word "pig" in Chinese is "**zhū**," since Orthodox __Jews__ aren't supposed to eat __pork__, which is not considered kosher!*

zhū is said with the first tone. Think of the high level back of a pig.

猪 This character has the "dog" radical on the left, which is the radical for the majority of characters for small and mid-sized mammals in Chinese. The phonetic on the right,

者, seems to show the sun on the bottom rising up above the earth at the break of day, which is when the pigs expect to be fed.

zhǔ 主 lord; ruler; owner

For us Christians, our <u>Lord</u> was a <u>Jew</u>. And the <u>owners</u> of many delis in New York City are <u>Jews</u>.

zhǔ is said with the third tone/low rising tone, as if vocally bowing down before your lord or master.

主 The ruler in ancient China was a king (王) who rose like a flame above his people, visible to all. The top stroke is the flame.

zhù 住 to live

Many <u>Jews</u> <u>live</u> in the Promised Land.

zhù is said with the fourth tone/falling tone, seeming to reflect the idea of settling <u>down</u> somewhere.

住 The character has the "people" radical on the left, indicating people residing in a certain location. The phonetic on the right is 主, the Chinese word for "lord." Servants in ancient China lived with their lord.

zū 租 to rent

*The danger when you <u>rent</u> an apartment or house is that the tenants might turn the place into a "zoo" (<u>**dzu**</u>)!*

zū is said with the first tone/high level tone, seeming to reflect the feeling of tenants that their rent is too high.

租 This character is written with the "grain" radical on the left, referring to the fact that tenant farmers in China always paid their rent by a percentage of their crops. The phonetic on the right is a double phonetic, sometimes read as *zu* or *cu*.

INDEX

STONE
BRIDGE
PRESS

Other Titles of Interest
from Stone Bridge Press
www.stonebridge.com

BOOKS BY LARRY HERZBERG AND QIN XUE HERZBERG

Basic Patterns of Chinese Grammar: A Student's Guide to Correct Structures and Common Errors

Chinese Proverbs and Popular Sayings: With Observations on Culture and Language

China Survival Guide: How to Avoid Travel Troubles and Mortifying Mishaps

"UNDERSTANDING CHINA THROUGH COMICS" SERIES BY JING LIU

Volume 1. Foundations of Chinese Civilization: The Yellow Emperor to the Han Dynasty (2697 BCE – 220 CE)

Volume 2. Division to Unification in Imperial China: The Three Kingdoms to the Tang Dynasty (220 – 907)

Volume 3. Barbarians and the Birth of Chinese Identity: The Five Dynasties and Ten Kingdoms to the Yuan Dynasty (907 – 1368)

ADDITIONAL TITLES

Chinese 24/7: Everyday Strategies for Speaking and Understanding Mandarin
by Albert Wolfe

Chinese Business Etiquette: The Practical Pocket Guide
by Stefan H Verstappen

The Pearl Jacket and Other Stories: Flash Fiction from Contemporary China
edited and translated by Shouhua Qi

Japanese Girl at the Siege of Changchun: How I Survived China's Wartime Atrocity
by Homare Endo; translated by Michael Brase